UNION INTERPARLEMENTAIRE

pour

L'ARBITRAGE INTERNATIONAL

SESSION DE 1904

COMPTE RENDU DE LA XIIᵉ CONFÉRENCE

TENUE À SAINT LOUIS, MISSOURI

DU 12 AU 14 SEPTEMBRE 1904

UNION INTERPARLEMENTAIRE

POUR

L'ARBITRAGE INTERNATIONAL

SESSION DE 1904

COMPTE RENDU
DE LA XIIᵉ CONFÉRENCE
TENUE À SAINT LOUIS, MISSOURI
DU 12 AU 14 SEPTEMBRE 1904

WASHINGTON
IMPRIMERIE NATIONALE
1905

UNION INTERPARLEMENTAIRE

POUR

L'ARBITRAGE INTERNATIONAL.

XIIᵉ CONFÉRENCE
TENUE À SAINT LOUIS, MISSOURI.

ORDRE DU JOUR.

1° Election du président et des vice-présidents.

2° Allocutions des délégués des groupes.

3° Proposition concernant la guerre actuelle. Rapporteur: M. le comte Goblet d'Alviella.

4° Développement des idées pacifiques; accords internationaux; progrès à réaliser dans ce domaine. Rapporteur: M. Gobat, conseiller national suisse.

5° Invitation aux puissances de convoquer une deuxième session de la conférence tenue à La Haye en 1899, pour délibérer sur les questions suivantes, savoir: (a) Les points ajournés par la conférence de La Haye; (b) La négociation de traités d'arbitrage entre les nations qui seront représentées à cette conférence; (c) l'opportunité de créer un congrès international qui se réunirait périodiquement pour discuter les questions internationales. Rapporteur: M. Burton, membre du Congrès des Etats-Unis.

6° Opportunité de la révision de la convention de Genève, spécialement au point de vue de l'emploi des explosifs et des dangers auxquels ils exposent les neutres. Rapporteur: M. le comte Albert Apponyi.

7° Protection de la propriété privée sur mer en temps de guerre. Rapporteur: M. Hepburn, membre du Congrès des Etats-Unis.

8° Moyen de renforcer l'action de l'Union interparlementaire. Rapporteur: M. Gobat, conseiller national suisse.

9° Rapport de l'administrateur du Bureau interparlementaire.

10° Nomination des membres du Conseil interparlementaire.

11° Epoque et siège de la prochaine conférence.

12° Imprévu.

PROJETS DE RÉSOLUTIONS.

Ad 3 de l'ordre du jour. La Conférence interparlementaire, émue par les horreurs de la guerre qui se poursuit en Extrême-Orient entre deux états civilisés et regrettant que les puissances signataires des conventions de La Haye n'aient pu avoir recours aux clauses qui les invitent à offrir leur médiation dès l'ouverture des hostilités,

Prie les puissances signataires des conventions de La Haye d'intervenir au moment opportun auprès des belligérants pour faciliter le rétablissement de la paix et charge le Bureau interparlementaire de porter la présente résolution à la connaissance des dites puissances.

Ad 4. La conférence exprime sa vive satisfaction au sujet du développement des idées pacifiques pendant l'année dernière, notamment de la conclusion de traités d'arbitrage entre la France et la Grande-Bretagne, la France et l'Italie, la France et l'Espagne, qui doivent être suivis de conventions d'arbitrage entre d'autres Etats; elle voit dans les accords récemment conclus entre la France et la Grande-Bretagne pour l'arrangement des questions coloniales qui étaient litigieuses depuis longtemps entre ces deux puissances, un événement heureux et important et invite les autres gouvernements à procéder de la même manière en supprimant, si faire se peut, d'un commun accord, des différends invétérés qui pourraient amener un jour de graves complications, s'ils n'étaient arrangés à temps par une entente mutuelle.

Ad 5. Considérant que l'opinion publique éclairée et l'esprit de la civilisation moderne exigent que les différends entre nations soient réglés de la même manière que les contestations entre individus, c'est-à-dire par des cours de justice et conformément à des principes légaux reconnus,

La conférence demande que les divers gouvernements du monde entier délèguent des représentants à une Conférence internationale qui devra se réunir à l'époque et au lieu désignés par eux pour délibérer sur les questions suivantes, savoir:

(*a*) Les points ajournés par la conférence de La Haye,

(*b*) La négociation de traités d'arbitrage entre les nations qui seront représentées à cette conférence,

(*c*) L'opportunité de créer un congrès international qui se réunirait périodiquement pour discuter les questions internationales,

Et décide de prier respectueusement et instamment le Président des Etats-Unis d'inviter toutes les nations à se faire représenter à cette conférence.

Ad 6. Considérant que la navigation et le commerce des Etats neutres souffrent un dommage et des inconvénients sérieux résultant de l'usage des mines flottantes dans les récentes opérations militaires, la conférence exprime le désir que les conventions concernant les usages de la guerre soient revisées en vue d'éviter les dangers dont il s'agit.

Ad 7. La conférence prie ses membres d'engager les parlements auxquels ils appartiennent à inviter les gouvernements à faire reconnaître par une conférence internationale le principe du droit des gens de l'inviolabilité de la propriété privée sur mer en temps de guerre.

Ad 8. Dans le but de renforcer l'action de l'Union interparlementaire, il est désirable:

(*a*) Que les groupes interparlementaires aient une forte organisation, qu'ils s'occupent spécialement des questions internationales et qu'ils concertent des actions préparatoires ou décisives dans leurs parlements;

(*b*) Qu'il soit reconnu que les membres des groupes interparlementaires sont, en vue des actions concertées, solidaires, sans distinction des fractions politiques auxquelles ils peuvent appartenir;

(*c*) Que les groupes interparlementaires répandent dans leurs parlements, traduites dans la langue du pays, toutes les communications qui leur seront faites par les organes de l'Union interparlementaire;

(*d*) Que l'Union interparlementaire ait un organe de publicité;

(*e*) Que le Bureau interparlementaire soit organisé de telle sorte qu'il puisse centraliser et coordonner tous les documents relatifs aux affaires diplomatiques et en communiquer des extraits utiles quand il le jugera nécessaire;

(*f*) Que le Bureau interparlementaire soit constitué en personne juridique.

Le Conseil interparlementaire est invité à exécuter immédiatement la résolution *f*, et pour le surplus, en tant que besoin, à soumettre des propositions à la prochaine conférence.

SÉANCE D'OUVERTURE DE LUNDI, 12 SEPTEMBRE 1904, FESTIVAL HALL
DE L'EXPOSITION, À 10 HEURES 30 DU MATIN.

M. GOBAT. Suivant l'article 7 des statuts, l'assemblée procède elle-même à la nomination de son président. Au nom du groupe américain et du Conseil interparlementaire, j'ai l'honneur de vous proposer M. Richard Bartholdt, membre de la Chambre des représentants du Congrès des Etats-Unis.

M. Bartholdt est désigné par acclamation comme président de la XIIe Conférence interparlementaire. Il prend place au fauteuil présidentiel.

Mr. BARTHOLDT. Gentlemen, I greatly appreciate the honor you have bestowed on me by my selection as your presiding officer, and on behalf of the American group I thank you. In calling the Twelfth Interparliamentary Conference to order, I bid you a cordial welcome in the name of the Congress of the United States.

I note the gratifying fact that 14 different countries of Europe are represented here, and, including the American Congress, 15 different parliaments of the world. Unlike other visitors, the 200 and more delegates, all of them actual members of national legislative bodies, have been attracted here neither by the wonders of the greatest of all expositions nor by mere curiosity to see the New World. They have traversed the thousands of miles now between them and their homes in the interest of an idea—on behalf of a great cause—the cause of humanity. We meet here to-day not as individuals riding a hobby to please our fancy, but as lawmakers clothed with authority by the votes of the people; and while we have not been expressly delegated by the people to serve the specific purpose which has brought us together, we feel that no grander service could be rendered any constituency anywhere under the sun than the service which would result in lessening the possibilities of war. We are pledged to render such service by creating a public sentiment, and by using whatever influence we may possess in the several legislative bodies to which we have been elected, in favor of law and justice in international relations as against brute force—in favor of right as against might. In other words, we ask—aye, we demand—that differences between nations shall be adjudicated in the same manner as differences between individuals are adjudicated—namely, by arbitration; by the arbitrament of courts in accordance with recognized principles of law rather than by war. Are we right? Surely! But war will continue, they say. True; we can not abolish it any more than we can abolish murder by enacting laws against it. But is this a good reason why we should not make laws against murder? Shall the fact that the sword is still being drawn deter us from entering agreements which, if faithfully carried out, will leave the sword firmly sheathed? Our skeptical friends know we are right; enlightened public opinion admits it; the cause of humanity is outraged by any other view. The goal of good government, after all, is the welfare and prosperity of the people, and it is because we know that peace surely promotes and war surely destroys that which statesmanship is supposed to strive for, that the friends of international arbitration urge the governments of the several nations to adopt this method of settling disputes, and thereby further the very objects of efficient statecraft.

Great and wonderful strides have been made of late years in the direction of a mode of settlement of international differences more in harmony with the demands of modern civilization. The Hague conference and The Hague court, scoffed at at first by wiseacres and skeptics, are no longer the objects of sneers. Religious wars are, fortunately, horrors of the past; wars for mere conquest will no longer be waged, and calls to arms to defend what is termed national honor are being too carefully scrutinized by enlightened and politically ripe nations to be resorted to without good and substantial reason. Does it not occur to you and to all that the dogs of war are being gradually starved to death?

We want the great powers to negotiate arbitration treaties among each other which will carry with them guaranties to the people of an era of peaceful progress and undisturbed development, and thus enable human instincts and faculties to exert their highest possibilities in the arena of art, science, and industry. We want to see The Hague court clothed with jurisdiction to arbitrate each difference between governments and nations, and we want an international legislature to consider and agree upon a universal code of law which is to govern the court's decisions and will tend to substitute for international anarchy a reign of law and order, an era of justice and peace.

The government which will take the lead in this movement will reap the plaudits and blessings of mankind; the country refusing to join it will stand convicted by public sentiment.

I rejoice in the presence here of the chosen delegates of so many nations. Your presence, I know, will be a new incentive to the American government to carry further the noble mission of this Republic, and thus rise to the full height of your expectations.

I now have the distinguished honor to present to you the honorable Francis B. Loomis, the first assistant Secretary of State, who will address you in behalf of President Roosevelt and the Government of the United States.

M. FRANCIS B. LOOMIS, sous-secrétaire d'Etat. Your presence here this brilliant September morning is agreeable evidence of the fact that the great cause to which you are so unselfishly devoted is neither dead nor languishing.

I am glad to welcome the delegates and members of the Interparliamentary Union to this city and to this country. The Government of the United States and its people are pleased to have you here. The President of the United States directs me to extend to you his kind and most cordial greetings. Valuing as he does the blessings of peace, earnestly desiring the diminution and lessening of the rigors and horrors of war, your coming is particularly grateful to him, for you are about to discuss phases of a problem of deeply human and world-wide interest—the peaceful settlement of international disputes.

You will find here, I think, a kindly and potent awakened public sentiment—a sentiment distinctly favorable to the widest practicable application of the principle of arbitration to the adjustment of international affairs where grave interests and issues are at stake, as well as to those of a less embarrassing nature which may be quite wholly composed through diplomatic agencies. You will find in this country, I am proud to say, a responsive and sympathetic environment. Your deliberations will be followed with warm and friendly interest by the American people, and every advance, every forward step you make toward a realization of those high ideals which inspire your councils and direct your labors, will receive the encouraging approbation and sincere plaudits of the American people, who cherish the hope that the world one day may enter upon the threshold at least of that blessed era, "the thousand years of peace."

For more than a century there has existed in this country a virile and steadily increasing sentiment in favor of the adjustment of differences between nations by some method less brutal and less costly than a resort to arms. This sentiment has found expression from time to time in treaties and conventions negotiated by the Government and in the creation of commissions to whom questions of international importance have been referred for adjudication. The work of these various tribunals and commissions will doubtless be of far-reaching consequence, because from it may be evolved a unified system of general principles which should appeal by their sanity, lucidity, fairness, and scientific derivation to all of the governments of the earth.

Within the last one hundred years there have been more than 200 cases in which international differences have been adjusted by the peaceful method of arbitration in one form or another, and the Government of the United States has been a party to about 70 of these arrangements. The most notable treaty in which this Government was concerned, and one which has had, perhaps, the most profound and beneficent results in that it has directed and powerfully influenced public opinion, was the treaty negotiated in Washington in 1871, which provided for four arbitrations. Of it Mr. John Morley says:

The treaty of Washington and the Geneva arbitration stand out as the most notable victory in the nineteenth century of the noble art of preventive diplomacy and the most signal exhibition in their history of self-command in two of the three chief democratic powers of the Western World.

The active good will of the American people and Government with respect to all practical efforts to give effect to the principle of arbitration was again splendidly and sufficiently demonstrated by the part which the American delegates took in the peace conference, and has been still further shown by the untiring efforts of this Government to contribute to the stability, permanence, and importance of The Hague tribunal. A former Secretary of State has well said:

It is especially gratifying to us Americans to know that our Government was the first to show its faith in the efficacy and utility of The Hague court by resorting to it, with our neighboring republic of Mexico, for the settlement of a question of long-standing diplomatic controversy. The result of that trial has encouraged us to continue to resort to it, and it has had a salutary influence on other of the signatory powers. We were a second time gratified at that action of our Government when President Roosevelt was asked by the three powers—Germany, Great Britain, and Italy—to arbitrate their differences with Venezuela. In place of accepting the responsible trust so flattering to his impartiality, he courteously declined and referred them to the court at The Hague, which had by them and us been created for just such cases.

It was a memorable event, which testifies to the progress of the world in the appreciation of reason as against force when those powerful nations stopped their coercive operations against a weak foe, recalled their navies, and agreed to submit their claims to arbitration commissions, and to refer to The Hague tribunal the essential questions involved in the conflict. * * * And it is a matter of just pride to us that this result was brought about by the action of the President of the United States.

Many private individuals have wrought well and valiantly in the field of international arbitration, and we do not forget that it was Andrew Carnegie, a generous American, who crowned a long line of noble, philanthropic work by giving to the world the Temple of Peace, a permanent and worthy abiding place for The Hague court.

In this connection I desire to compliment the Interparliamentary Union upon the declaration which it made at its conference held in Holland in 1894 in favor of a permanent court of arbitration and the subsequent development of its plan for such a court, prepared by a commission of six members appointed for that purpose. The Interparliamentary Union deserves credit for practically forecasting five years in advance what proved to be the most salient work of the peace conference at The Hague. Several members of the Interparliamentary Union were delegates to that conference and exerted strong and important influence upon its action and decisions. I congratulate the members of the Union upon the substantial and gratifying progress which has been made, largely through their steadfast and intelligent efforts since the organization of this body some fifteen years ago. Great results have been achieved, and have been achieved quickly. You have aroused, directed, and educated public sentiment in favor of arbitration throughout the civilized world. Your work will still be in this direction. The Union should never cease its efforts to stimulate public interest in arbitration. It is this force which we call

,public opinion, or public sentiment, which is the court of last resort—the power that rules the world. It directs the actions of men in all communities and in all forms of society; it compels a certain measure of civilization, a certain measure of respect for law; it determines what shall be the form and purpose of government; it regulates manners and customs; it is more potent than potentates; it is superior to constitutions, for it overthrows and changes them. Governments, perhaps more than individuals, are dominated and modified by it; its sway is universal; "it sweeps the earth and it touches the stars."

If the opinion of the world shall be aroused and vivified and permanently concentrated in a formal demand that war shall cease the realization of your ideals would indeed seem to be at hand.

The last year has been rich in achievement. The cause of international arbitration is making notable and permanent progress. Since your last meeting Great Britain and France, France and Italy, Great Britain and Italy, Holland and Denmark, Great Britain and Spain, France and Spain, France and Holland, and Spain and Portugal have concluded treaties pledging themselves during a period of five years to submit certain classes of cases to The Hague Tribunal. The signing of these treaties marks a distinct and promising advance. It is not too much to prophesy that within five years all of the civilized nations of the earth will enter upon similar treaty obligations. The Alaskan boundary dispute has been amicably settled, and the record of the year counts among its achievements, besides the cases dealt with in The Hague Tribunal, the appointment of special arbitrators to settle—

The Japanese house tax case, between Japan and France, Great Britain and Germany.

The boundary dispute between Ecuador and Peru.

The boundary dispute between Colombia and Peru.

The claims for indemnity of French citizens on the treaty shore of Newfoundland, arranged under the general agreement between France and Great Britain.

The question of the boundary line at the entrance of the Christiana Fiord, between Sweden and Norway.

The land question in the New Hebrides, between France and England.

The Barotzeland frontier question, between Great Britain and Portugal.

The differences between the Turkish Government and the administration of the Ottoman debt.

Also the San Salvador and Dominican Republic arbitrations were brought to successful issue.

It is the earnest hope of the President of the United States that at no distant day the path may be made clear for entering into a comprehensive agreement of arbitration with all governments which share our views. This matter is having at present the most earnest consideration. The Government of the United States, in all proper ways, will continue to give its aid and encouragement to the cause of international arbitration, to which it is so firmly and earnestly committed.

This is a significant and memorable gathering. It marks an epoch in the cause so dear to your hearts. There has never been before in the New World an assemblage similar to this in character, composition, and aims. You are legislators chosen and ordained to give law to the civilized peoples of the earth. You have great powers, great opportunities, but it behooves you to remember that your responsibilities are coequal and commensurate with them. You represent law-abiding and liberty-loving people. Our most precious possessions came to us as a heritage. The men of to-day have not to fight for freedom of thought, or of speech, or of action, as their ancestors did; but if we enjoy the blessings of freedom which they won for us, let us not forget that there are those in every country to whose perverted minds and unawakened consciences liberty means little more than freedom from restriction, disloyalty to law, and the right to harass and prey upon organized society. Wheresoever liberty lifts her gracious, serene, and noble countenance to-day, back of it, like a horrid specter, glares the forbidding, sinister, and ignoble apparition of license and anarchy.

It occurs to me while we attune our voices to pæans in praise of liberty and peace those of us who may be intrusted with the duty of making laws for the nations of the world might properly pause to consider also what legal remedies, outside the sphere of diplomacy, treaties, and arbitrations, can be devised and applied to the settlement of questions arising from the consideration of such serious international problems as anarchist assassins, general sanitation, emigration and immigration, and citizenship. Here, I think, is a wide, varied, and important and immediately practicable field which may very well invite your most solemn and strenuous endeavors.

Commingle with your efforts in behalf of international arbitration and the coming of an era of concord among the nations a conscientious and intelligent effort to promote peace and good will among individuals, to compose class differences, to eradicate class hatreds, to bring about social order. The sources of power must be purified. Unless the individual can be enlightened and uplifted I fear there can be no such thing as profound international peace or a very long-continued practice of settling anything more than the most trivial differences among nations by resort to arbitration.

The rapidly growing interest in the subject of international arbitration indicates, however, that your educational endeavors are not in vain; that they are bearing fruit; that they are well directed. It is

not necessarily to be believed that all of the wishes and all the dearest
and completest ideals of those who hope for universal peace and universal disarmament may be realized. Still, nothing in the realm of
moral endeavor seems impossible; and while the way seems long and
the difficulties almost insuperable, yet by hard and sensible work and
earnest and prayerful striving you may so animate, inspire, and uplift
those who follow you that the latter may have the glorious fate to live
in the golden time when the war drums throb no longer and the battle
flags are furled—

"In the Parliament of man, the federation of the world."

M. DAVID R. FRANCIS, président de la compagnie de l'exposition.

I esteem it a privilege to bid you a cordial welcome here in behalf
of the management of the Louisiana Exposition. In this day war is
a mere contest between appliances of science, not prowess; and the
wealth of a country also determines its ability to win its battles.
Therefore, for the sake of justice, causes should be settled by arbitration. It is fitting that such a congress as yours should assemble on
the grounds of this universal exposition, for this exposition also is a
great promoter of peace. It brings together in friendly rivalry every
nation of the globe. It facilitates acquaintances and promotes a mutual
good feeling. An exposition of this character lessens the circumfer-
ence of the globe, and makes it more difficult for nations which have
differences to settle them by arms. I again bid you welcome.

Il est procédé ensuite à la nomination des vice-présidents. Sont
désignés: MM. Hauptmann, membre de la Chambre prussienne des
députés; le chevalier Wladimir de Gniewosz, député au Reichsrat
d'Autriche; Houzeau de Lehaie, sénateur de Belgique; v. Krabbe,
vice-président du Folkething danois; Burton, membre de la Chambre
des représentants du Congrès des Etats-Unis; Cochery, député français; Stanhope, membre de la Chambre des communes de la Grande-
Bretagne; le comte Apponyi, député hongrois; le marquis di San
Giuliano, député italien; Lund, ancien président du Lagting norvégien; Tydeman, député aux Etats Généraux des Pays-Bas; de Paiva,
ancien député portugais; le général Pilat, de Roumanie; Beckman,
député suédois; Gobat, conseiller national suisse.

M. BARTHOLDT, président. Je donne maintenant le parole, dans l'ordre alphabétique français des pays qu'ils représentent, aux délégués
des différents parlements.[a]

M. HAUPTMANN (Allemagne). Da ich in folge der Anordnung des
französischen Alphabets die Ehre habe, als erster der Delegaten der
verschiedenen Gruppen zu sprechen, so benutze ich die Gelegenheit,
um, bevor ich auf den eigentlichen Gegenstand meiner Rede eingehe,

---

[a] Les discours des représentants de la Belgique et de la Hongrie n'ont pas été remis
au secrétariat.

den Vereinigten Staaten von Nord-Amerika unseren wärmsten Dank
für die grossartige, geradezu fürstliche Aufnahme auszusprechen, die
Sie uns hie bereitet haben. Ich bin allerdings nicht beauftragt, im
Namen aller hier anwesenden Mitglieder der Interparlamentarischen
Friedenskonferenz das Wort zu führen, aber ich glaube doch den
Empfindungen Aller Ausdruck zu verleihen, wenn ich sage, dass der
Empfang, den man uns in Amerika bereitet hat, hoch erhaben ist über
allem, was die kühnste Phantasie sich hätte einbilden können. Man
darf es mit Recht behaupten, dass die Interparlamentarische Friedenskonferenz noch niemals unter solchen Verhältnissen getagt hat, als es
jetzt der Fall ist. Man sagt oft, wenn die Amerikaner etwas thun,
thun sie es immer grossartig. Wir durften hiernach viel erwarten,
aber unsere Erwartungen sind weit übertroffen worden. Sie haben
uns nicht nur hier in der gländzendsten Weise aufgenommen, sondern
Sie haben und wollen uns auch noch weiter die Gelegenheit geben, die
weitgedehnten Gefilde, die hochentwickelte Industrie, das rastlose
Vorwärtsstreben dieses Landes in einer solchen Weise kennen zu
lernen, wie es einem Privatmann niemals möglich ist, wie es nur der
Fall sein kann, wenn man die Ehre hat, der Gast einer so grossen
Nation zu sein, wie die Ihrige es ist.

Nehmen Sie dafür unseren wärmsten, aufrichtigsten Dank entgegen.
Was man uns hier geboten hat, werden wir nie vergessen. Und wenn
unsere Aufnahme hier alles in Schatten gestellt hat, was uns bisher
entgegengebracht worden ist, so Vieles und so Schönes es auch war,
dann glaube ich auch behaupten zu dürfen, dass ebenso in Zukunft die
Gastfreundschaft, die die Vereinigten Staaten uns erwiesen haben, von
keinem andern Lande übertroffen werden wird.

Was die Thätigkeit der deutschen Gruppe angeht, so hat dieselbe
der Hauptsache nach sich auf die stille Propaganda beschränken müs-
sen. Es ist das ein Weg, der nicht durch die breite Oeffentlichkeit
führt, auf dem aber oft mehr erreicht wird, als in lärmenden Ver-
sammlungen. Und mancher Stimmungswechsel, der plötzlich sich
vollzieht, ist auf diesem Wege vorbereitet worden. Vorurteile werden leichter zerstreut in einem Gespräch, wo die Einwendungen des
Gegners widerlegt werden können, als in einer Rede, in der man
vielleicht zufälligerweise das nicht berührt, was diesem bedenklich
scheint und wo er Aufklärung wünscht. Und darauf kommt es heute
vor allem an, die Gegner aufzuklären, umzustimmen, für uns zu
gewinnen. Gerade der Parlamentarier kann hier erfolgreich wirken,
der Parlamentarier, der so oft Gelegenheit hat, mit einflussreichen
Leuten zu verhandeln, denen unsere Ideen utopische, unausführbare
scheinen. Die andere Aufgabe, die Freunde, die Anhänger, zusam-
menzuhalten, liegt mehr in dem Wirkungskreise anderer Vereinigun-
gen. Und das dürfen wir sagen, meine Herren, dass unsere Ideen
Fortschritte machen. So von vornherein ablehnend, wie früher, ver-
hält man sich uns gegenüber doch nicht mehr. Auf diesem Wege

werden wir fortfahren und in stiller, emsiger Arbeit für unsere grosse Sache wirken.

Vielleicht darf ich Ihnen noch mitteilen, dass wir in dem preussischen Abgeordnetenhause eine Bibliotek von Werken der Friedenssache eingerichtet haben. Der langjährige verdiente Sekretär der deutschen Gruppe, Herr Dr. Hirsch, den Krankheit zu seinem und unserm innigen Bedauern verhindert hat hier zu erscheinen, hat seine wertvolle diesbezügliche Büchersammlung hier deponirt. Es is mir eine angenehme Pflicht, auch hier unsern warmen Dank für diesen hochherzigen Entschluss ihm auszusprechen. Ich brauche nicht erst hervorzuheben, von welchem Werte es ist, wenn gerade in Parlamenten diese Werke immer zur Hand sind, und ich möchte den Mitgliedern der andern Gruppen anheimgeben zu erwägen, ob bei ihnen ähnliche Massregeln nicht auch sich als nutzbringend erweisen würden. Ich schliesse, indem ich resumire, dass wir Fortschritte gemacht haben, dass unsere Ideen sich immer weiter verbreiten und unsere Sache immer mehr Anhänger findet, so dass wir frohen Mutes in die Zukunft sehen können.

M. DE GNIEWOSZ (Autriche). Il existe en Autriche plusieurs nations qui, quoique réunies sous le sceptre de la dynastie de Habsbourg, forment cependant autant d'individualités jalouses de leurs droits historiques, c'est pourquoi je dirai d'abord quelques mots dans leurs différents idiomes, et d'abord en polonais, en ma qualité de Polonais, fier de l'histoire millénaire de ce royaume de Pologne, qu'un acte de brigandage a détruit. [Suit la traduction en langue allemande.]

Die Polen haben in Nord-Amerika gewisse alte Verdienste, denn der polnische Held Taddée Kosciuszko kämpfte im Unabhängigkeits-Kriege neben Washington für die Befreiung Amerika's von englischer Herrschaft, wurde zum General ernannt und wegen seiner Tapferkeit und militärischen Erfolge mit dem Cincinnati-Orden von Washington geschmückt.

Auch jetzt sind in Nord-Amerika beinahe 2 Millionen Polen, welche meist als Arbeiter in den Bergwerken und Fabriken, so wie auf Farmen, schwer arbeiten und gute, ruhige Bürger sind.

Diese empfiehlt Redner der Obhut und dem Wohlwollen der Amerikaner und dem hochverehrten Herrn Präsidenten Roosevelt.

[Puis l'orateur prononça quelques paroles en tchèque, en slovaque, en croate, en serbe et en italien et continua en allemand.]

Dass Oesterreich für die Idee der Schiedsgerichte ist, und seine Reichsvertretung, beweist die Theilnahme am Schiedsgericht in Haag und der festliche Empfang der interparlamentarischen Union im Jahre 1903 in Wien durch die Regierung Körber's und die Hauptstadt Wien, u. s. w.

Vor allem ist unser allergnädigster und bester, ungemein beliebter Monarch Franz Joseph I. für den Frieden, wie er dies, nicht in Worten, sondern in Thaten oft bewiesen hat.

Mit seinen Gegnern im Norden und Süden, mit denen er blutige
Kriege in den Jahren 1848, 1859 und 1866 um seine ererbten Rechte
als Kaiser von Deutschland und um zwei Provinzen in Italien führen
musste, schloss er in edelmüthiger Weise bald nachher ein Friedens-
bündniss. Ist das nicht zu bewundern? Als er während des deutsch-
französischen Krieges Gelegenheit hatte, seine Rechte zurück zu
gewinnen, hielt er, wie er versprach, strenge Neutralität ein. Ebenso,
während des russisch-türkischen Krieges, da es den Russen bei Plewna
so schlecht erging und er seine ärgsten Feinde leicht ungemein
schwächen und vernichten konnte, blieb er neutral, wie er es versprach. Auch jetzt hat er, der Erhaltung der Ruhe und des Friedens
wegen am Balkan, mit Russland ein Uebereinkommen getroffen, wie
dort Ordnung zu schaffen wäre und hält daran fest, obgleich jetzt nach
den schrecklichen Niederlagen Russland's in Ost-Asien, Gelegenheit
wäre, Oesterreich's, Einfluss und Suprematie dort einzuführen.

Darum kann der Kaiser von Oesterreich-Ungarn mit Recht der
Friedenskaiser par excellence genannt werden und alle Welt muss ihn
als solchen verehren und lieben.

Auch die oesterreichische Regierung ist für die Idee der Schiedsgerichte, sowie der gemeinsame Minister für Oesterreich-Ungarn für
äussere Angelegenheiten, Agenor Graf Goluchowski, oft eingetreten;
besonders hat der oesterreichische Minister-Präsident Ernst von Körber bei der Eröffnung der Versammlung der Interparlamentarischen
Union in Wien 1903 in einer glänzenden Rede diesen Tendenzen leb-
haften Ausdruck gegeben, und auch die Mittel zum Empfang der
hohen Versammlung der Abgeordneten aller Parlamente bereitwillig
bewilligt (48,000 Kronen) und die freie Fahrt auf allen Staatsbahnen;
der Kaiserliche Hof überliess den Vertretern der interparlamentarischen Union das Kaiserlich-königliche Hof-Opernhaus zu einer Fest-
vorstellung und Erb- Graf Harrach empfing mit Gemahlin die Gäste
festlich in seinem alten herrlichen Palaste in Wien.

Der Bürgermeister der Reichshauptstadt Wien, Dr. Carl Lueger,
bewirthete und feierte die Gäste im Prachtsaale des monumentalen
Rathshauses mit einem grossartigen Gastmahle. Im oesterreichischen
Parlament sind beiläufig fünfundsechszig Abgeordnete Mitglieder der
interparlamentarischen Union, auch aus dem Herrenhause gehören
hoch angesehene Mitglieder der Union an, als Graf Schönborn, Professor Dr. Lammasch, Excellenz von Plener, gewesener Finanz-
Minister, der so ausgezeichnet und würdevoll die Berathungen der
Union voriges Jahr führte und eine Hauptstütze unserer Bestrebungen
sein wird. Im Abgeordneten-Hause haben auch mehrere Herren für
das internationale Schiedsgericht als obligat gesprochen. So Dr.
Herold, Dr. Russ, Dr. Kramarz, Baron Kübeck, Professor Dr. Four-
nier, Dr. Lueger, Dr. Roszkowski, Gniewosz, u. s. w. Doch das ist
alles zu wenig, wenn nicht das Schiedsgericht obligat sein wird. Wir

haben unter dem Vorsitze des Baron Pirquet mehrere Sitzungen abgehalten und nahmen an allen Congressen Theil.

Bei dieser Gelegenheit muss ich noch ganz irrthümliche Meinungen über Oesterreich, die ich in Amerika hörte, berichtigen—das ist, dass Oesterreich dem Verfalle nahe sei.

Meine Herren, Oesterreich wird immerdar bestehen und wie der grosse czechische Patriot Palacki sagte, ebenso der grosse Begründer des deutschen Kaiserreiches Fürst Bismarck sich äusserte (ob aufrichtig, weiss ich nicht): wenn Oesterreich nicht wäre, so müsste es geschaffen werden. Die Völker Oesterreichs streiten zwar im Parlament über die Rechte ihrer Sprache oft recht hitzig und heftig, aber dieselben Völker wandern auch nach Amerika aus und leben hier mit einander in Frieden und Freundschaft.

So wird es auch im Momente der Gefahr in Oesterreich sein. Alle Völker werden für ihren geliebten Kaiser und sein Reich einmüthig einstehen und jeden Feind mit aller Kraft bekämpfen.

Deshalb schliesse ich mit den Worten: Unser vielgeliebter Kaiser lebe hoch noch lange Jahre als der beste Hort des Friedens!

M. von KRABBE (Danemark.) Dans le courant de cette année le monde, spectateur d'une guerre acharnée, a eu du moins la satisfaction de voir conclure plusieurs traités préventifs contre des guerres futures.

Chargé de faire ici le rapport du Danemark, je suis heureux de pouvoir dire que ma patrie a conclu un traité d'arbitrage en principe des plus avancés, et par cela même assez remarquable.

L'essence de ce traité est qu'il ne soustrait aucun cas possible à l'arbitrage ni à la sentence de la Cour de La Haye.

L'univers a applaudi un traité d'arbitrage entre la France et l'Angleterre. C'était un fait glorieux, un progrès éminent. Mais pour garantir la solution pacifique de tous les différends entre deux nations, il reste beaucoup à faire.

Le traité anglo-français n'a trait en effet qu'aux différends d'ordre juridique ou relatifs à l'interprétation de traités. D'autres traités entre d'autres nations contiennent les mêmes restrictions, ainsi le plus récent, celui entre l'Allemagne et l'Angleterre.

C'est à ce sujet que la convention signée à Copenhague, le 12 février 1904, entre les Pays-Bas et le Danemark a un très réel mérite. Elle statue, sans détours et sans restrictions, que ces deux Etats s'engagent à soumettre à la Cour permanente d'Arbitrage tous les différends et tous les litiges entre ces deux Etats qui n'auront pu être résolus par les voies diplomatiques.

Le 9 décembre 1902, la Chambre des députés du Danemark avait voté, sur la proposition de notre groupe, une invitation au gouvernement de pourvoir à ce que dans tout traité entre le Danemark et un autre Etat soit insérée la stipulation que les différends occasionnés par les traités seront soumis à la Cour de La Haye.

Non seulement le gouvernement a donné suite à cette sommation, mais il a en outre étendu cette idée dans la convention danoise-hollandaise.

Aussitôt que le Parlement des Pays-Bas aura approuvé la convention, les ratifications seront échangées à La Haye.

Nous croyons que la conclusion de traités comme le danois-hollandais prêche d'exemple.

Il est regrettable que l'on croie devoir distinguer ici entre les grandes puissances et les petites. On prétend que les vastes intérêts d'une grande puissance ne lui permettent pas de soumettre à l'arbitrage tout litige international. Mais si les intérêts d'une grande puissance sont d'une considérable étendue, l'étendue des malheurs de la guerre d'une telle puissance est en proportion.

Espérons qu'il entrera dans la politique même des grandes puissances de soumettre tous leurs différends à la Cour de La Haye, sans aucune restriction.

A ce point de vue, la convention danoise-hollandaise contient un autre article lumineux. C'est que tout Etat non signataire pourra adhérer à la convention par une simple notification faite aux Etats contractants.

Mais le principal, ce qui mérite toute votre attention, c'est cet article qui soumet à la Cour permanente de La Haye, sans réserve aucune, tout différend que les moyens diplomatiques n'auront pu aplanir.

C'est dans cette voie, Messieurs, qu'est l'avenir.

Au nom du groupe danois, je remercie cordialement nos frères américains de nous avoir invités et reçus d'une manière si splendide et de nous avoir permis de nous rassembler sous le drapeau étoilé, symbole heureux de la grande République des Etats-Unis, qui marche vers la victoire à l'avant-garde pour faire triompher la cause de l'arbitrage international.

M. BARROWS. (Etats-Unis). It is a welcome task to come as the bearer of good tidings which announce the progress of international peace achieved through international justice.

The progress of our cause has been marked in the last year by three events in which the Government of the United States has been a participant and a factor.

The first event, and one of great importance, was the settlement of the Alaskan boundary question between Great Britain and the United States. This question was a heritage of the acquisition of Alaska by the United States by purchase from Russia in 1867. It involved complicated historical and geographical questions, just those questions of delimitation which in the past had been a prolific source of war between nations. The general coast line of Alaska, not counting intricacies, is 4,750 miles long, or 855 miles longer than the general coast line of the United States on the Atlantic and the Gulf from

Maine to Texas. So long as the vast district of Alaska remained undeveloped a theoretical boundary line answered the purposes of the cartographer, but with the influx of settlers to that country following the discovery of gold the necessity of a practical and final settlement of the question of boundary was appreciated by Canada and the United States, as well as by the home Government. It was therefore agreed that this question should be referred to a Commission composed of members appointed by Great Britain and the United States.

The Commission was composed of six members, three of them citizens of the United States, two of them citizens of Canada, and the sixth the president of the Commission, the lord chief justice of England. The case was argued by eminent counsel on both sides. The Canadian and United States Commissioners divided on the main points of issue, but the vote of the lord chief justice favored the paramount claim of the United States.

A story is told of an Englishman who came to Boston and, seeing the Bunker Hill monument, playfully taunted a Boston young lady on having a monument which commemorated the defeat of the Americans in the battle of Bunker Hill. The young lady modestly replied: "Yes, you won the battle, but we got the hill." In the Alaskan boundry dispute it is the United States again that has got the land; but Great Britain has won a splendid victory, a victory which attests the integrity and supremacy of the English conscience. In subordinating national considerations and interests to his interpretation of international obligations, the distinguished English jurist has given a noble illustration of judicial impartiality. It is not difficult to think of a time in the past when such a thing would have been impossible. Great Britain comes out of this dispute with an ethical dignity and grandeur which must command the admiration of the world. Truly, righteousness exalteth a nation. What nobler form can our patriotism take than a high and undeviating sense of national obligation? What progress we shall have made when every nation shall be as scrupulously careful in respecting the most minute obligation to another nation as it is in defending its own rights and its own territory.

The second event is familiar to members of this conference, for the United States was but one of eleven nations which appeared before the great international tribunal, The Hague court, to settle a question of preferential claims in the Venezuela case. The position of our own nation among the suitors had, however, a certain significance from the fact that the President of the United States had been asked by the blockading powers to act as arbitrator in the question at issue. President Roosevelt, however, as you well know, declined the honor and urged that the question be submitted to The Hague court. In taking this position the President, I am confident, secured not only the approval of public sentiment in the United States but also the approval of the advocates of international arbitration throughout the world. The United States, which, with the sister Republic of Mexico, had presented the first case of international difficulty to The Hague court, availed itself of this second opportunity to recognize the competence and validity of that tribunal.

With the result of that decision you are all familiar, and I need not recite its terms. It is sufficient to say that the court did not take up the question of the validity of the claims or the method adopted for their collection by the powers preferring them; it confined itself to a question of contract made by Venezuela with the three blockading powers, Great Britain, Germany, and Italy, to the effect that if they would remove the blockade, 30 per cent of the revenues of two designated ports would be applied to the payment of their claims in preference to the claims of the seven other powers, Belgium, France, Mexico, the Netherlands, Spain, Sweden and Norway, and the United States.

The court recognized the obligation involved in this contract, and decided that Great Britain, Germany, and Italy should have preference over the other creditors in the liquidation of these claims. The popular surprise and disappointment at the decision disappeared when the legal aspects of the case were reviewed by some of our eminent lawyers. Judge Gray, president of the Mohonk conference of international arbitration, a jurist of international distinction, who has represented the United States at The Hague court, maintained that the decision could not have been otherwise.

Another event, and it seems to us of great importance, in the development of the sentiment for international arbitration, was the formation of a group of the Interparliamentary Union in the Congress of the United States. Its organization we owe most of all to the indefatigable efforts of the president of this congress, Hon. Richard Bartholdt. That more of the members of our group are not present at this conference is explained not so much by the vast distances, in our country, whose magnitude you yourselves are beginning to measure, as by the fact that we have entered upon that interesting and exciting quadrennial event, the contest of a Presidential election. This absorbs the time and energies of many of our representatives.

The main purpose of the Interparliamentary Union is to avoid war through arbitration rather than to discuss the ethics of war. But you will agree, the most of you I am sure, with our early philosopher and statesman, Benjamin Franklin, that it is of the utmost importance to diminish the number and force of the motives for war; and this conference has twice approved by resolution the position which Benjamin Franklin so early took and which has been the traditional position of our country concerning the inviolability of private property at sea in time of war. In this connection I am sure it will be of interest to announce to this conference another step taken by the United States, not of an international character, but which is of the greatest importance in diminishing the force of those motives which lead to war. I refer to the abolition of prize money as a method of compensating its naval officers in time of war. This step was taken by the Congress of the United States soon after the Spanish war, at the close of the session of 1899. It has not before been announced to this body. Indeed, the step was taken so quietly that a large number of people in our own country did not and do not yet know that it has been taken. It was accomplished without the slightest agitation, and was the result of the sentiment of our naval officers, who no longer wish to secure remuneration in this way—no longer wish to rest under the imputation of desiring war for the sake of their share of the spoil resulting from the capture of the enemy's goods.

Under whatever name we may disguise it, the giving of prize money is a relic of Homeric times, when the spoil of the enemy was divided among the victors. It is a relic of piracy, in which soldiers and sailors fought for the booty they could make out of their enemies.

The other day on our excursion up the Hudson River, our escort, the *Topeka* of the United States Navy, was gayly dressed with flags and gave a salute in honor of this Interparliamentary Union. It was with much personal satisfaction, I assure you, that our officers could participate in that event. As I watched those flags on the *Topeka*, the occasion seemed to me to have moral significance, because one flag had been hauled down. From remote antiquity there had come down to us a pirate flag. It was not visible among our symbols, but it floated in the consciousness and expectation of our sailors. That pirate flag has been hauled down, never again to be raised. An eminent naval writer, not of our own country, has defended the division of spoil as providing a stimulus and motive for war which nothing else can supply. I am happy to say that our naval officers to a man have set aside as unworthy this motive for war, and that in doing so the United States has ranged itself with most of the enlightened nations of the world.

M. Cochery (France). C'est à nos amis, MM. Labiche et de La Batut, vétérans des conférences interparlementaires, qu'il appartenait de prendre la parole au nom du groupe français.

En vous transmettant leurs excuses de ne pas être aujourd'hui au milieu de nous—des raisons de force majeure les ont retenus en France à la dernière heure—je tiens à dire tous nos regrets de leur absence, regrets partagés par tous ceux qui savent leur dévoûment infatigable à la cause de l'Union interparlementaire.

Les événements écoulés depuis la dernière conférence ont facilité ma tâche.

Ce n'est pas d'efforts ou d'espérances, mais de résultats acquis que j'ai à vous entretenir.

Depuis la dernière conférence, la France a conclu un traité d'arbitrage avec l'Angleterre, un traité d'arbitrage avec l'Espagne, un traité d'arbitrage avec l'Italie, un traité d'arbitrage avec la Suède.

Sans doute, ces traités ne réalisent pas tout notre idéal, ils ont besoin d'être complétés, étendus. Mais le plus difficile c'était de faire le premier pas: il est fait. Des traités d'arbitrage sont conclus.

En même temps, une entente cordiale avec nos amis et voisins du Royaume-Uni de la Grande-Bretagne et d'Irlande faisait disparaître dans un arrangement général tous les germes de difficultés entre les deux pays et dissipait les nuages qui pouvaient obscurcir la vision nette des aspirations communes et des intérêts communs des deux peuples.

Ces résultats ne sont pas le fruit d'une improvisation. Ils ont été préparés par le mouvement des esprits, par une nouvelle orientation des idées due à l'Union interparlementaire. C'est à l'Union interparlementaire qu'il faut en faire honneur.

Le succès couronne tant de persévérance et de généreux efforts.

Des réunions comme celle-ci ne remuent pas seulement des idées généreuses et ne posent pas seulement des problèmes que la diplomatie considère d'abord comme insolubles et finit ensuite sous le souffle de l'opinion par résoudre; elles préparent d'une façon immédiate des solutions en établissant un contact périodique des membres des divers parlements.

C'est là le principal objet et aussi le plus immédiat résultat de nos réunions.

Dans ce contact, les préventions disparaissent, les sympathies naissent, on apprend à mieux se connaître, à mieux s'estimer; des idées communes surgissent et l'on s'aperçoit que des hommes de bonne volonté, animés de pensées généreuses, même lorsqu'ils les expriment dans les langues les plus diverses, arrivent rapidement à se comprendre.

Aussi vos conférences nous laissent toujours le souvenir d'une rencontre pleine de charme et de résultats importants et pratiques.

Nous avons eu, avec vos collègues du Parlement anglais, la bonne fortune d'éprouver le même sentiment il y a quelques mois: le Parlement anglais a reçu à Londres les membres du Parlement français et le Parlement français a reçu à Paris les membres du Parlement anglais.

C'est un exemple à suivre, et nous comptons bien que des semblables visites réciproques entreront dans les traditions parlementaires.

Le temps n'est plus, en effet, où les secrets de la diplomatie règlent seuls, souvent à leur insu, les relations et les rapports des peuples. Les peuples sont devenus majeurs et savent régler eux-mêmes leurs relations au gré de leurs sympathies, de leurs intérêts, de leurs affinités. Des courants s'accusent plus forts que les combinaisons les plus savantes de la diplomatie; ces courants préparent les solutions que les diplomates n'ont qu'à inscrire sur le parchemin.   Aujourd'hui, ce sont les peuples qui ouvrent la voie; la diplomatie constate et régularise.

Pour nous, nous constatons avec une grande joie une pareille évolution; nous applaudissons avec enthousiasme aux résultats qu'elle prépare.

Fils de la Révolution française, nous ne pouvons être indifférents à aucune idée généreuse et nous saluons avec enthousiasme tout ce qui peut apporter plus de fraternité, plus de progrès, plus de bien-être à l'humanité.

M. Stanhope (Grande-Bretagne). The custom that has prevailed at the annual conferences of the Interparliamentary Union of calling upon each group to justify its existence by a record of its activities and accomplishments during the preceding year has generally been to many of us a cause of much embarrassment. It was often humiliating to admit how small had been the harvest which we had been able to reap, and we were generally confined to showing how sedulously we had planted the seed and how hopeful we were with regard to the future.   On this occasion, however, it is most gratifying to record substantial advance, and, as president of the British group, to be permitted to refer to the practical steps that have been taken to give increasing effect to the principle of international arbitration.   During the past year treaties of arbitration have been completed between Great Britain and the following countries, viz: Germany, Italy, Holland, Belgium, and Sweden and Norway, while a great convention between Great Britain and the French Republic has, we hope, settled for all time every outstanding cause of difference between our two countries.

It is meet, indeed, that this conference should be assembled upon the soil of the United States of America, in a land consecrated to the noblest ideals of progress and of humanity.   Here in this atmosphere of freedom it is possible to give the fullest expression to our aspirations and our ideals.   We may, indeed, be far distant from that day which shall proclaim the permanent establishment of universal peace, but the sacred precept which tells us to strive for "Peace on earth and good will toward men" must always stimulate us to go forward in our efforts and gradually awaken the conscience of mankind, and thus prepare the way for the establishment of that reign of justice which we hope is destined to supplant the horrors of bloodshed and the dread arbitrament of war.   I may be pardoned if I refer with some pride to the labors in this field of my own compatriots, to the inspiring oratory of Cobden and of Bright, and, above all, to the noble eloquence of Gladstone, and if I also venture to remind you that the names of these men of our race are illustrious alike in both hemispheres, and are the common glory of all branches of the Anglo-Saxon people.

Assembled as we are to-day in such large numbers, drawn from so many parliaments and from such.great distances, to jointly labor in a cause that unites us all, it is but natural that I express in the first place the heartfelt gratitude of the British group, in whose name I here speak, for the splendid welcome which has been extended to us by the President and people of the United States, and also should emphasize the hope, to which allusion has already been made by every preceding speaker, that our labors this year may be signalized by a notable advance in the great cause which our union has been established to maintain.

M. DI SAN GIULIANO (Italie). L'orateur expose en langue anglaise tout ce que l'Italie a fait depuis la dernière Conférence pour la cause de l'arbitrage international et de la paix. Il rappelle les traités d'arbitrage signés par l'Italie avec la France et la Grande-Bretagne, et les glorieuses traditions de son pays, parmi lesquelles il signale l'arbitrage entre les Etats-Unis et la Grande-Bretagne, concernant le litige de l'Alabama, qui a empêché une guerre imminente, arbitrage confié à un tribunal dont un Italien, le comte Sclopis, fut le président. Il exprime le désir que les Etats-Unis et l'Italie marchent toujours au premier rang dans le mouvement pour la justice internationale.

M. LUND (Norvège). Some nine hundred years ago my countrymen, the Norsemen, under the leadership of Leif Erikson on one of their many adventurous raids found their way to America, and in memory of this event a statue has been erected to Leif Erikson in Boston. A record of his deed was afterwards found in the old Iceland Sagas, and the fact was possibly well known to America's later discoverer, Columbus.

In Leif Erikson's time my countrymen did not understand enough to put their great discovery to use. The expeditions of the Northmen were in those days more to Britain, to France, to Italy, and even to the ancient Byzantine town, Constantinople. Everywhere they gathered honor and booty, and to a certain extent founded settlements, as in Britain, Normandy, and other lands.

However, the Norsemen, too, since the foundation of the United States, have known how to appreciate the worth of America, and now for generations thousands upon thousands of Norway's sons and daughters have gone forth year by year to win from her virgin soil a reward of their labors, such as the old country with its harder, sterner nature could not afford them, in spite of all the love it bore to its own.

Some one and a half millions, or more than half of Norway's inhabitants, here beneath the Star-Spangled Banner and under American free institutions, that so much resemble Norway's, have found for the most part happiness and wealth. And I use this occasion to-day to express to you the good wishes and thanks of the old country for the hundreds of thousands of happy Norse homes which America has bestowed upon our children.

There is a sort of floating bridge between the United States and Norway. The emigrants go out, and then come back constantly in thousands to visit the old homes of their fathers. There they tell of this land of adventure, and then return again, followed often by new recruits.

But in spite of all the youth and strength that wanders away, the old land must still try and maintain its place and live its own life. And I am glad to be able to tell you that despite all struggles and difficulties old Norway has still continued to go on.

There has been a long pause in the development of our country. Far back in the middle ages we certainly occupied a respected place among the peoples. As evidence of Norway's culture, we may name our Saga literature, and point to visible memorials in our Trondhjem cathedral and our King's Hall at Bergen.

But times changed, and for Norway there came a long period of inertness, lasting through hundreds of years. Since Norway, in 1814, obtained a free constitution, our land, although amidst many struggles, has yet steadily advanced. In our practical daily life, as is well known, the shipping industry of Norway may be reckoned among the greatest of the world; in art, science, and literature I can quote names like Ibsen, Bjornsen, Edward Grieg, and Nansen. Our land seeks, indeed, the noblest ideal of all, to fulfill her modest part in the general work of civilization.

And in this cause, which has specially brought us here together in the work for peace and arbitration, Norway has, according to its means, sought to yield its contribution. Since the Interparliamentary Union was established our land has been represented at nearly all the conferences. From the first, before any other State, the Norse Storthing, the body which in our land votes supplies, has granted traveling allowances to its representatives at the conferences. The Norse Storthing was the first to sanction a considerable contribution to the Central bureau in Berne of this organization, and has since that time besides voted an annual contribution, not only to this bureau but also to the International Peace Bureau at Berne.

Norway was among the very first European nations to try and bring about permanent treaties of arbitration with other lands. I am glad to be able to inform you that our present foreign minister seems just as warmly interested in the matter as his predecessor, more than half a score years ago, when the Norse Storthing first raised the question, showed himself cold and indifferent to it. We are now negotiating regarding permanent arbitration treaties with ten different lands, and some of these treaties are being brought to a successful conclusion.

I have dwelt so particularly upon these details, both because our land, its history and its effectiveness, thanks to our special political circumstances, are at present little known abroad; and because I think this also is evidence that even a small country like Norway can give its mite to the advancement of civilization in general and to the greatest question of our time, the work of peace, if it is allowed to live its own independent life in accordance with its means and the circumstances under which it has been set in the world.

For the little work which Norway has undertaken in the service of peace, or perhaps I should say for the good will which in this respect is shown, our land has already got special recognition. Our neighbor Sweden's great son, Mr. Alfred Nobel, has, as is well known, intrusted the Norse Storthing with the task of bestowing a yearly prize—about 150,000 francs—upon the person or persons who by competent work in the cause of peace have earned distinction. This prize has now been already conferred in three consecutive years.

Mr. President, it is with feelings of exceeding pleasure and gratitude that the Norse representatives here this year visit this conference. Not alone because we thereby get occasion to express our good wishes to the land that has bestowed happy homes upon so many of our children, but also because we are enabled to declare our thanks for the great work America, before any other land in the world, and already from the past century's first decades, has carried out in the interests of peace. Names like Channing, Elihu Burritt, and many others, down to American men and women of our own day, stand out, as it were, like signposts and milestones on the great high road of peace.

And further, but lately this year and in this city the United States has established a record, and I doubt not that its action will leave deep traces behind. Time after time have we at the interparliamentary conferences called upon the press of the world to unite with us, in our work. At The Hague a motion was proposed on the subject in warm-hearted eloquent words by our highly respected and so recently departed comrade the former French ministei of justice, Mr. Traieux. Again in Paris in 1900 Hungary's gifted speaker, our esteemed colleague, Count Apponyi, in a brilliant speech delivered a fresh appeal to the press, but all in vain. Now at the Congress of the World's Press, recently held here, with the full support of America's great statesman, Mr. John Hay, the cause of peace was placed on the international peace programme. The European representatives who met readily gave in their adhesion to the idea. And I am convinced that the United States will do its best hereafter to make the fourth estate the world over a loyal, steady ally in the fight.

I feel no doubt that America, that has so long and so efficiently striven for the mission of peace, will also plight her honor to carry on the same to a fuller completion, to the lasting benefit of herself and all mankind.

M. Tydeman (Pays-Bas). The Holland delegation salutes the Twelfth Interparliamentary Conference most cordially. I am commissioned to bring you kindest greetings from its absent members, and especially from our chairman, the zealous cooperator of so many conferences, our excellent friend, Mr. Rahusen.

I must speak to you about our group and its activity for the cause of peace in our country. I am glad to be able to tell you the group is perfectly well. The number of its members has greatly increased—comparatively speaking, the greatest of all—about two-thirds of the total of our parliament. In Holland the cause of arbitration is advancing from day to day, and in the same measure we are reinforcing our army and navy. We are proceeding with the simple and purely logical idea that only international arbitration will be able to stop the crying expenses for armaments, crying indeed, as I can tell you. The expenditure for army and navy amounts this year to exactly 25 per cent of our total budget, 44,000,000 florins, which should be employed for public education, for developing means of transport, and in combating pauperism. Unluckily we have not yet reached that point. The famous "si vis pacem para bellum" of our celebrated Grotius is still valuable. We are still obliged to stop at the threshold of the temple which should bear this inscription on its façade: "Si vis pacem para justitiam."

Nevertheless, I am glad to be able to mention three milestones that have loomed up on our way since our conference in Vienna.

First. The general and obligatory treaty of arbitration concluded with Denmark, signed at The Hague, October 14, 1903. This treaty is remarkable as being the first that I could call a perfect or complete treaty of arbitration, because it does not contain the usual restrictive clause for all causes which concern the vital interests, the independence, or the sovereignty of the contracting States, the caoutchouc clause which opens the door for exception and escape. You will not be astonished when I say that the absence of these usual restrictions aroused some objections in our Parliament—objections not at all founded, because neither the honor nor vital interests of a State can be injured by a jurisdiction tending neither to humiliate, nor to debilitate, nor to destroy State or people, but to reinforce and maintain them.

In the second place, I must call attention to the general treaty of arbitration concluded by our Government with France, signed April 8, 1904. This treaty is conceived on the same terms as the Anglo-French treaty. As is known, the usual restrictions are augmented by the clause that all causes which concern the interests of third, not contracting states, are excepted from arbitration and put out of the limits of the treaty.

It seems to me that although the conclusion of a general treaty of arbitration between England and France, two of the great powers of Europe, is of the greatest importance, it will not be favorable to the furtherance of arbitration if this treaty becomes the type of future ones.

Thirdly. I can give you the latest particulars as to the donation of your generous fellow-citizen, Andrew Carnegie, who most liberally provided the permanent court of The Hague, with the means of establishing a home and library, a gift which once more proves how closely the idea of international arbitration is joined with the logic and clever initiative sense of the American.

The Dutch Government has carried out, according to the statutory letter of the donator, the regulations of the donation. The directors are appointed and made subordinate to a superior council, composed of the ministers in office and some high public officials. The committee is now in full activity and occupied with the plan of establishing a building worthy of its destination. The selection of the site offers some difficulties because everyone is meddling, but soon the battle of the architects, the battle of the arts of peace, will be fought.

I would point out the immense importance of the fact that our twelfth conference meets here, on American soil, the part of the globe, formerly called the " New World." For, Mr. President, there is no longer a new world—there is only one world, and that is the whole world. Formerly politicians concerned themselves with European equilibrium. Now this is far behind us. Henceforth we shall have to occupy ourselves with the maintenance of the political equilibrium of the world.

We are now the sorrowful spectators of a cruel struggle between two nations. Russia has its frontiers in the center of Europe; Japan, in the extreme Orient, reaches its right hand over the Pacific to the continent of North America. The geographical situation of the two struggling nations is sufficient to explain my thoughts. Henceforth the great and powerful Republic of the United States will have to play an important rôle in the world's policy.

I feel happy over this circumstance, because the United States rests on the basis of peace. Its leading men are imbibed not with the idea of war, but with the sense of peace and justice. Your First Magistrate, your eminent President, has attached his name to the international arbitration, and it was he who first submitted a case to The Hague court.

We all, representatives of the parliaments of Europe and America, intrust to you, the American people, the sacred cause of arbitration.

Once more: My heartiest greetings, sincerest wishes, in the name of the Holland delegation, to the conference of St. Louis!

M. DE PAIVA (Portugal). Depuis longtemps je souhaitais de visiter l'Amérique, non seulement parce que son histoire se rattache à celle de mon pays, mais parce que, pour le monde ancien, l'Amérique est, pour ainsi dire, la terre promise, et pour ce qui me concerne particulièrement, parce qu'un de mes grands-pères était américain.

Je viens de réaliser mon souhait, et je n'ai pas lieu de m'en repentir; bien au contraire, je suis charmé de la manière captivante dont vous venez de recevoir vos hôtes, les apôtres de la paix; et par ce que j'ai vu, je pourrai dire, et je vous en assure, à mes concitoyens, que cette nation n'est pas seulement grande par son étendue, par ses richesses, par ses industries, par ses beautés, par ses plaines et ses montagnes, par ses fleuves et ses lacs, par ses villes et les parcs qui les entourent, par ses musées et monuments, par ses écoles et universités, par sa délicatesse, son bon sens, son patriotisme; par ses inventeurs, tels que Edison; ses historiens, tels que Bancroft; ses romanciers, tels que Fenimore Cooper; ses poètes, tels que Edgar Poe, mais surtout grande, très grande, par son amour pour la paix internationale!

Elle a mis en évidence la haute considération qu'elle professe pour l'idéal pacifique, par l'invitation qu'elle a adressée aux membres de l'Union interparlementaire de se rassembler ici; par les statues de la paix qui s'élèvent belles et gracieuses dans l'exposition; par l'accord maintenu depuis plus de trois-quarts de siècle, avec le pays voisin, le Canada, au sujet de l'absence complète de soldats, de navires de guerre et de fortifications sur les 4,838 kilomètres de rivage qui séparent les Etats-Unis de ce pays, par le recours à l'arbitrage dans plusieurs différends internationaux, par sa Philadelphie, la ville des amis de la paix, et par ses innombrables sociétés de la paix qui travaillent incessamment pour la propagation des principes concernant la justice internationale.

Elle nous fait espérer que, pour l'avenir, elle continuera à être un des facteurs les plus puissants, sur lequel pourra compter notre idéal pour devenir une réalité. Et pour le croire, il ne faut que vous rappeler que c'est Monsieur Roosevelt qui a été le premier à indiquer aux puissances le tribunal de La Haye pour la solution des litiges internationaux, et que c'est un autre de vos illustres présidents, Monsieur Harrison, qui a dit: "La circonspection, la justice et la dignité doivent caractériser notre diplomatie; une diplomatie intelligente doit être disposée à faire prévaloir le principe d'un arbitrage amical dans les conflits entre particuliers, et de même, à terminer pacifiquement au moyen de l'arbitrage les différends internationaux. C'est par ce procédé que nous contribuerons à la paix du monde."

Tout cela nous prouve que dans l'esprit de ce très grand, très noble, très puissant pays existe l'idée de la paix internationale; car s'il n'en était pas ainsi, il n'aurait certainement pas choisi pour décorer cette salle le drapeau qui porte cette noble devise: "Paix à toutes les nations!" Tous les peuples aiment et respectent leurs drapeaux; pour l'avenir vous défendrez votre idéal aussi courageusement que vos drapeaux.

De cette façon le nom des Etats-Unis du Nord, déjà très brillant, sera béni par toutes les nations du monde, puisqu'il représentera un élément des plus importants du progrès de l'humanité par le droit, et du bonheur des peuples par la paix. Je le salue donc respectueusement!

Pour ce qui concerne mon pays, et pour m'acquitter du devoir que, d'après nos statuts, le conseil m'a imposé, je suis heureux de pouvoir vous affirmer que, depuis la dernière conférence jusqu' à présent, il a continué à travailler comme auparavant pour le progrès de notre idéal.

La presse est presque entièrement de notre côté; quelle que soit sa couleur politique, elle défend notre cause et publie volontiers les faits qui intéressent le mouvement pacifique.

La Ligue portugaise de la Paix continue à faire de grands efforts pour notre idéal au moyen de son journal, de ses publications, de ses messages, de ses conférences, de ses séances solennelles devant un grand concours d'assistants. Parmi ses résolutions s'en remarque une suivant laquelle un de ses membres serait chargé d'écrire et de publier un livre de propagande pour être distribué gratis à toutes les écoles du pays, et une autre, consistant à faire à outrance la guerre au duel, et à présenter à ce sujet au Parlement un projet de loi. Parmi ces différentes publications, il y a un petit mais très intéressant travail de Monsieur le comte de Penha Garcia, *Le Portugal et l'arbitrage*, dont la Ligue offre aux membres de la Conférence 400 exemplaires, que je vous prie, Monsieur le président, de faire distribuer.

Dans le premier établissement scientifique du Portugal, l'ancienne et très remarquable Université de Coimbra, Monsieur le docteur Villela, illustre professeur de droit international et un des membres les plus éclairés et les plus vénérés de la Faculté de Droit et de la Ligue portugaise de la Paix, ainsi que du groupe parlementaire de la paix, et ancien député, a exposé à ses élèves les idées les plus pures au sujet de de notre idéal; et ses leçons exubérantes d'érudition et de vigueur logique, et constituant un livre de 1,000 pages à peu près, le signalent comme un ardent apôtre de la paix internationale, digne de notre vénération la plus profonde. Je vais envoyer à notre bureau de Berne un exemplaire de ce livre, afin qu'il puisse être consulté par ceux qui s'intéressent à la cause de la paix.

Dans le Parlement, c'est la Haute Chambre elle-même qui a pris cette année l'initiative de nommer officiellement les membres du groupe de l'Union interparlementaire en les choisissant parmi les Pairs du Royaume les plus distingués. Je remets à notre honorable secrétaire la liste officielle, imprimée, des 65 membres du groupe. Malheureusement, ils n'ont pu se rendre ici à cause d'une séance extraordinaire du Parlement portugais qui a lieu en ce moment.

Dans le gouvernement, on remarque un courant également favorable; non seulement il a soumis à la décision arbitrale quelques-uns de ses litiges avec d'autres pays, mais il a conclu un traité d'arbitrage avec l'Espagne, qui a resserré davantage les nœuds qui unissent les deux pays voisins. Je viens d'envoyer à notre bureau un exemplaire de ce traité et des messages adressés à ce sujet par la Ligue portugaise au gouvernement de mon pays et au ministre d'Espagne ainsi que de la réponse.

Certainement, il y a dans mon pays un amour enraciné pour la cause de la paix. Ce ne sont pas seulement les poètes et les philosophes qui soutiennent les principes de notre credo, mais les hommes publics, les hommes positifs et pratiques. Le grand ministre d'Etat, Monsieur Anonio de Serpa Pimentel, disait, dans le Livre Blanc de 1892: "L'arbitrage est une institution dont le but est de maintenir la justice dans les relations internationales, sans humilier les petites puissances devant les grandes puissances; et le Portugal a toujours professé le vœu le plus sincère que les différends, sur lesquels on ne peut pas s'accorder, soient résolus au moyen de l'arbitrage."

Le grand homme d'Etat Andrade Corvo, dans son étude sur les provinces d'outremer, disait: "On ne peut pas continuer à vivre dans le siècle actuel de même qu'on vivait aux XVI^c et XVIIe siècles. Le monde a changé, il faut savoir changer avec le monde; et ce qui était utile, admissible il y a deux siècles, est aujourd'hui absurde, nuisible et inacceptable; alors le commerce était la guerre, aujourd'hui c'est la paix."

Le Directeur général de l'instruction publique, le docteur Abel d'Andrade, dans son livre, "*Principe des Nationalités*," a dit: "La guerre est condamnée par la voix de l'humanité, et le temps n'est pas éloigné où la garantie des nationalités sera aussi efficace que celle des droits individuels."

Le professeur Villela dans son livre sur le droit international ajoute: "Les Etats modernes ont atteint une communion d'intérêts si intense et une mutualité de relations si constante que, en exerçant en commun une longue autorité, ils sont arrivés à constituer une nouvelle forme, à laquelle on a donné le nom de Société des Etats ou de Communauté ou Societé internationale; et l'arbitrage est le moyen juridique de résoudre les conflits, le moyen d'organiser la paix juridique vers lequel doit tendre naturellement l'esprit humain."

Le Portugal a traduit ces idées dans les conventions internationales. Par exemple, l'article 6 de la convention avec l'Etat Indépendant du Congo, de 1841, dit: "Les hautes parties contractantes conviennent, pour le cas où elles n'arriveraient pas à s'accorder directement, à recourir à l'arbitrage d'une ou de quelques puissances amies pour la résolution des différends qui pourraient surgir après la signature de la présente convention." L'article 16 du traité avec la Suède et la Norvège, de 1895, dit: "En cas de divergence sur l'interprétation ou sur l'application du présent traité, qui ne puisse pas être réglée au moyen de la correspondance diplomatique, les deux parties contractantes s'accordent à soumettre le différend au jugement d'un tribunal arbitral, dont elles s'obligent à respecter et à exécuter loyalement la décision." L'article 7 de la convention avec les Pays-Bas de 1894, dit: "Tous les différends ou désaccords sur l'interprétation ou sur l'exécution de la présente déclaration, de même que tout autre différend qui pourrait surgir entre les deux pays, à condition qu'il n'intéresse pas leur indépendance ou leur autonomie, seront soumis au jugement de deux arbitres, nommés par chacun des deux gouvernements. En cas de divergence entre les deux arbitres, ceux-ci choisiront, d'un commun accord, un tiers-arbitre qui décidera."

Ce sont donc les hommes d'Etat, les représentants des gouvernements, les gouvernements eux-mêmes qui témoignent par leurs actes de la confiance qu'ils ont dans la paix par l'arbitrage.

Moi-même, juge de Droit, voyant chaque jour les plus grands potentats se courber devant la majesté de la loi et respecter les décisions de la justice, je ne peux qu'être un croyant, un ardent apôtre de la paix par le droit. Voilà pourquoi j'ai cherché à établir dans mon pays un courant aussi fort que possible en faveur de notre idéal, et dans ma dernière conférence au siège de la Ligue portugaise de la Paix, dont je viens d'offrir quelques exemplaires aux très illustres membres du Conseil, j'ai exprimé ma profonde conviction que le temps est arrivé où la parole est à la justice pacifique, où elle est arrachée à jamais à l'anarchie internationale, qui n'en a que trop abusé jusqu'ici. L'impossible d'hier, c'est la réalité de demain, sous la puissante main du progrès.

Les parlements s'entendent là-dessus au moyen de l'Union interparlementaire; les gouvernements par les conférences intergouvernementales; les nations par les traités d'arbitrage.

Il était indispensable que les nations finissent par se convaincre que leurs différends peuvent être résolus au moyen de l'arbitrage, et les faits viennent démontrer que cette conviction est enfin acquise; il fallait que le recours à l'arbitrage devint assez fréquent, et l'histoire contemporaine nous en offre de nombreuses applications, ce qui fait voir qu'on profite de plus en plus de ce moyen de dirimer les litiges; il fallait encore que les nations fussent prêtes à se soumettre aux décisions prises par les arbitres, et aucun cas n'est venu prouver qu'elles aient cherché à se dérober à leurs engagements vis-à-vis des arbitres choisis; il était, de plus, indispensable que les nations civilisées proclamassent la solidarité internationale et le respect pour l'état juridique international, et tout cela a été proclamé par ces mêmes nations civilisées dans la Conférence de La Haye, quand on y disait: "Que les gouvernements reconnaissent la solidarité qui unit les membres de la société des nations civilisées; qu'ils souhaitent d'étendre les domaines du droit et de fortifier le sentiment de la justice internationale; qu'ils sont animés du ferme désir de concourir pour le maintien de la paix générale, et que c'est dans les principes de l'équité et du droit que se fondent la sûreté et le bonheur des peuples." Il était finalement indispensable qu'un tribunal international fût chargé de résoudre les différends internationaux, et voilà qu'on peut dire aux pays civilisés que ce tribunal existe déjà, le tribunal de La Haye, composé d'arbitres aussi respectables par leur savoir et par leurs talents que par leur rang et l'intégrité de leur caractère, auquel les nations peuvent dorénavant confier la décision de leurs litiges.

Certainement Proudhon disait une vérité quand il affirmait que "L'humanité ne veut pas la guerre!" Le développement dans la société internationale, d'institutions positives, correspondant aux besoins sociaux, c'est un phénomène normal, c'est une conséquence nécessaire de l'évolution, de cette loi invincible qui se moque de tous les préjugés qui fait la civilisation, et qui a une alliée dans la conscience de chaque homme.

Notre cause est gagnée. Ce n'est pas moi qui le dis,—je suis suspect parce que je suis un croyant,—mais le journal La Gironde, qui n'est pas suspect puisqu'il tournait en ridicule nos efforts, les efforts de Monsieur le baron d'Estournelles, et voici ce que ce journal vient de dire dans un de ses derniers numéros, celui du 24 août: "Ce qui importe c'est de constater la force du courant qui entraîne la diplomatie. Qui l'eût prévu il y a seulement quelques années? Qui n'eût souri aux prétentions d'un doux philosophe demandant à faire passer dans le domaine des faits les rêveries humanitaires de l'abbé de Saint-Pierre? Et à la vérité, qui ne souriait aux campagnes de M. d'Estournelles de Constant? Et pourtant nous voilà témoins de l'aboutissement de ces campagnes."

Certes, notre cause est gagnée, je vous en félicite! Mais il faut marcher encore et marcher avec persévérance et fermeté pour que le triomphe soit complet. Travaillez, et à l'avenir l'humanité, plus heureuse qu'aujourd'hui, parlera avec respect et reconnaissance de l'Union interparlementaire, de même que je prononce aujourd'hui avec respect et reconnaissance les noms illustres de MM. Cremer et de Passy qui ont fondé cette institution; de M. Gobat à qui elle doit assurément la continuation de son existence, parce que c'est lui qui a guidé ses pas depuis son enfance; de MM. Houzeau, Descamps, Beernaert et tant d'autres, dont le talent et les efforts ont fait de l'Union interparlementaire une institution de la plus grande portée pour l'évolution la plus glorieuse de l'humanité, l'évolution du droit international.

Je rentrerai bientôt dans mon pays, où, selon Humboldt, l'immortel Colomb a principalement appris ce qui, en science et en pratique, lui a été le plus profitable; dans mon pays, où, d'après les paroles d'un grand orateur contemporain, on a commencé à fondre les clefs dont le grand navigateur devait se servir pour ouvrir aux yeux stupéfaits du monde le sanctuaire de la divine Amérique, dans mon pays qui, pendant huit siècles, a représenté sur la terre une Iliade de triomphes et sur la mer une Odyssée de gloires, dont l'histoire contient des pages intéressantes au sujet de la paix et dont le présent inaugure un nouveau courant de vie, de moralité et de progrès, indice certain d'une nouvelle phase de prospérité, et je lui dirai que dans mon cœur existera toujours le doux souvenir de la réception si grandiose de l'Amérique, et que dans mon esprit qui admirait déjà ce très noble, ce très puissant pays, brillera le doux espoir qu'il continuera à être un des champions les plus dévoués de l'idéal pacifique, et qu'un jour viendra où, à côté de la statue de la Liberté illuminant le monde, pourra être érigée celle de la paix protégeant et rapprochant les peuples dans une union fraternelle. Travaillez! Poursuivez!

M. PILAT (Roumanie). Je suis heureux d'accomplir, au nom du groupe interparlementaire roumain, un des plus agréables devoirs, en exprimant au gouvernement de la grande République Américaine nos plus vifs remercîments pour la gracieuse et grandiose hospitalité qu'il a bien voulu donner aux membres du Congrès interparlementaire.

Après les éloquents discours prononcés à cette tribune par les illustres orateurs qui m'ont précédé, il serait présomptueux de ma part d'abuser de votre patience, en exposant à mon tour les généreuses idées, les irréfutables principes et les vœux si profondément sentis par nous tous en faveur de la paix universelle.

J'avoue, Messieurs, avec grand regret, que dans notre pays nous n'avons pas produit des œuvres théoriques qui puissent servir les vues du congrès, faciliter ses travaux et qui méritent de retenir votre attention; cependant, dans notre position géographique, situés comme nous sommes, dans le voisinage de cette partie de l'Europe où des complications et des excitations belliqueuses menacent à chaque instant de compromettre la paix, nous avons su, par une attitude correcte et loyale, seconder les fins pacifiques de la diplomatie européenne.

Je le répète, si nous n'avons pas produit des œuvres importantes en faveur de la paix, nous avons, du moins, pratiquement collaboré à l'œuvre de pacification des esprits, en vue de prévenir des conflits qui auraient pu dégénérer en une conflagration européenne.

Aussi notre attitude sincèrement pacifique a-t-elle été hautement appréciée par les grandes puissances limitrophes, qui ont reconnu les services que nous avons rendus à la cause de la paix.

Je souhaite que les travaux du congrès atteignent le but tant désiré par nous tous, afin que, par des arbitrages internationaux, tous les conflits dangereux soient aplanis et qu'une paix heureuse assure le bonheur des peuples.

M. BECKMAN (Suède). Count Apponyi in his eloquent speech a few minutes ago said that a year is a very short time, indeed, in which to report progress in a cause so important as ours. It is true a year is but a second in the life of nations, but it has been well said by a French author that a second is enough for the seed to reach the soil where it may take root and where it may grow up into the mighty tree that gives shade and shelter to generations.

In the history of arbitration in our country this year has been most important, short as the space may be. For the first time in our diplomatic history we have concluded an obligatory treaty of arbitration. It was concluded with France in July, 1904. The form was analogous to that of the "declaration" between France and England. A few weeks later this arbitration treaty was followed by another with Great Britain.

Again, I may add that our Government, through the department of foreign affairs, has opened negotiations for the conclusion of arbitration treaties with Holland, Belgium, and Denmark. This year we are further to enter into negotiations with Spain, Portugal, and Switzerland, and somewhat later with this great country, the United States of America, and with the American Republics.

This is progress indeed, showing how the idea is rooting in the political life of our country. Let me note one thing more concerning these treaties. You all know the clause waiving arbitration in case the difference involves "the vital interests, the national honor, or the independence" of the high contracting parties. This clause is evidently a most elastic one. It can not, however, practically under present conditions be eliminated. Another way must be found to restrict its being used to too great an extent. We are hoping that at least in some of the above-mentioned treaties may be introduced an additional clause enumerating certain categories of cases concerning which the contracting parties agree not to make use of the clause of exceptions. That should, it seems to me, also imply progress of practical importance.

As to public opinion in our country, it is steadily growing, not only in favor of arbitration, but in the decided view that we can not live without arbitration, and that it is the duty of every people, great or small, to do its share of the peaceful work of the nations. From all our country, from the workman's home and the palace of the King, there is heard but one voice, and Oscar II, who has the right to be called a peacemaker, as he has had more than once the honor to be the arbitrator between nations, has just authorized me to express to this assembly of the Interparliamentary Union his best wishes for the success of our work.

I will not any longer trespass on your patience; but one word more you will, no doubt, allow me to add. As one of the representatives of Sweden, I wish to express to the people and the Government of the United States the heartiest thanks for the hospitality without bounds which you are showing us. Important in itself has this hospitality to me a special deeper meaning as an expression of the strong faith of your country in our work. We must remember that the tribunal at The Hague, historically, is a daughter of these interparliamentary conferences. Great was, therefore, the satisfaction of the members when the diplomatic conference at The Hague brought its work to a successful end. But when we saw with joy and hope that great institution looming up on the horizon there were many even among the true friends of arbitration who said, with misgivings and ill-foreboding: "That tribunal is in itself a noble structure, but what will be its fate? Believe us, it will stand without work, with closed doors, an empty hall." But who was it, gentlemen, that dispersed these fears? Who was it that first knocked at the doors and had them flung open and bade the tribunal begin its grand work of peace? It was "the first citizen" of this country, the President of the United States, who knocked in the name of the nation, and therefore I see in your noble hospitality to the members of the Interparliamentary Union a sign that the same spirit is still reigning, that the same faith in the necessity and the final victory of arbitration is still ruling in the mind of your nation.

In the name, therefore, of the Swedish group of our beloved old country, thrown up far away on the top of the globe, in the name also—I venture to say that, too—of the new Sweden, which we have everywhere around us, where many thousands of our countrymen have found happy homes—in the name of all of us—I beg to tender your people, your Congress, and your Government the expression of our everlasting gratitude.

M. Gobat. (Suisse). Comme représentant d'un pays neutre qui vit en paix avec tout le monde, dont la politique ne l'expose à aucun conflit avec d'autres Etats, et qui suit à l'extérieur comme à l'intérieur stricte-ment les règles du droit, je ne puis vous exposer pour la Suisse de grands travaux dans le domaine des aspirations de l'Union interparlementaire, ces aspirations formant pour ainsi dire l'essence de notre vie publique et de nos sentiments à l'égard de toutes les nations. Aussi, n'aurions-nous rien à apprendre de l'Europe. Quant au pays dans lequel nous nous trouvons, c'est une autre question. Beaucoup de gens m'ont dit, depuis que la Douzième Conférence interparlementaire est fixée: Comment l'Union interparlementaire, qui est avant tout une ligue européenne, peut-elle aller siéger en Amérique, la grande rivale de l'Europe? Eh! vraiment, les Etats-Unis, avec tant d'autres républiques américaines, qui tôt ou tard noueront avec eux des liens plus étroits, sont une puissance redoutable pour la vieille Europe. Ici, dans le Nouveau Monde, tout est en progrès et en pleine expansion; là, de l'autre côté de l'Océan, nous voyons la stagnation, sinon le recul; ici, le pays s'enrichit immensément; là, les Etats s'appauvrissent; ici, pas de soldats; là, poussé jusqu'à la folie, le système abrutissant des armées permanentes; ici, l'épargne se met tout entière au service de l'industrie, du commerce et de l'agriculture; là, elle sert à augmenter les dettes que les Etats accumulent pour leurs déplorables fantaisies militaires.

Depuis une dizaine d'années se dessinent de nouveaux courants économiques, qui placent les Etats-Unis à cent coudées au-dessus de l'Europe. Oui, ce pays est une puissance redoutable pour nous Européens. Eh bien! le danger auquel il nous expose, je l'aime; je le salue; je désire qu'il aille toujours croissant, parce qu'ainsi la jeune Amérique inculquera à la vieille Europe la sagesse qui manque à celle-ci. L'adversité est pour les nations comme pour les individus le grand éducateur. Je vois, dans l'avenir, grâce à la concurrence américaine, je vois surgir en Europe une organisation politique semblable à celle qui a fait des Etats-Unis le plus grand pays du monde.

Gentlemen of America, I come from a very old Republic, which for many centuries, was the only one in the world. Our political institutions are the same as yours; our State organization is the same as yours; our political liberties are founded, as yours, upon free individual movement, upon decentralization, and upon the cooperation of single States for mutual welfare. However, I envy the United States, not because the younger sister is much larger than the older one—for even a small State can be great—but because the United States does not belong, like Switzerland, to a system of States, the first purpose of which is to spend not only their own money, but also that which they have not, for military folly.

Gentlemen, I bring you the most cordial greeting of Switzerland.

Toutes ces allocutions sont accueillies par des applaudissements.

Le Président remercie les orateurs pour les paroles aimables qu'ils ont prononcées à l'égard des Etats-Unis et annonce que la prochaine séance aura lieu dans le Hall des Congrès.

La séance est levée à 1 heure 30.

SÉANCE DE MARDI, 13 SEPTEMBRE 1904.

La séance est ouverte à 11 heures du matin par le président.

M. Gobat. Je propose d'adresser au chef de l'Etat dans lequel siège actuellement la Conférence interparlementaire, le télégramme suivant:

The Twelfth Interparliamentary Conference, composed of representatives of fifteen different Parliaments at the commencement of its deliberations, sends its respectful and cordial salutations to the President of the Great American Republic. It considers itself fortunate to have the opportunity of holding its sessions in a country whose Chief Magistrate is considered by all nations a champion of international justice.

Cette proposition est acceptée par acclamation.

M. Gobat. L'assemblée voit que le service du secrétariat se compose de ma seule personne. Dans ces conditions, et comme je devrai en outre parler plusieurs fois, je ne puis prendre que des notes très sommaires. Je prie donc les orateurs de me remettre ici, ou de m'envoyer plus tard à Berne, leurs discours in extenso ou en résumé.

Le Président met en délibération le No. 3 de l'ordre du jour.

M. le comte Goblet d'Alviella, sénateur de Belgique. En développant devant vous la proposition à laquelle le bureau de l'Union interparlementaire a bien voulu accorder l'appui de sa haute autorité, je crois actuellement inutile de rechercher quelle peut avoir été la part de responsabilité incombant aux diverses Puissances européennes dans les événements qui ont amené la guerre entre le Japon et la Russie. Un seul sentiment peut prévaloir parmi vous au sujet de cette guerre. Elle doit nous être odieuse, d'abord parce que c'est une guerre, et une guerre entre des nations civilisées qui pourraient mieux employer leurs forces; en second lieu, parce qu'elle donne lieu à des hécatombes humaines, dont l'éloignement nous empêche seul de réaliser l'étendue et l'horreur; ensuite, parce qu'elle peut entraîner les conséquences les plus désastreuses, non seulement en Orient, mais encore en Occident, pour l'avenir de la civilisation.

Jusqu'ici, ce n'a été qu'une guerre entre deux Etats. Pour peu qu'elle se prolonge, elle risque de devenir une guerre entre deux races, c'est-à-dire la forme de guerre la plus envenimée et la plus désastreuse. Au début, le Japon a formulé des prétentions très modérées; il s'agissait uniquement de préserver l'intégrité territoriale de la Chine et d'ouvrir la Mandchourie au commerce de toutes les nations. N'y a-t-il pas lieu de craindre que, exalté par l'orgueil de ses victoires, non moins que par le sentiment de ses pertes et de ses sacrifices, le Japon ne finisse par se croire investi d'une mission providentielle et ne finisse par pousser le cri "l'Asie aux jaunes," en entraînant la Chine à sa suite? Voilà ce qu'il faut éviter à tout prix, non dans l'intérêt exclusif de la race blanche, mais dans celui de la paix du monde, et les gouvernements qui veulent sincèrement cette paix doivent être les premiers à comprendre l'urgence de la médiation que nous réclamons.

Ensuite, il y a toujours le danger que des puissances européennes ne soient entraînées à prendre part dans le conflit, et sans insister sur ce point délicat je crois pouvoir me faire ici l'écho des appréhensions qui se sont déjà fait jour dans la presse. Il y a de par le monde des mines toutes chargées; il suffit, pour y mettre le feu, d'une étincelle, comme il en peut jaillir à tout instant, d'une conflagration qu'il sera difficile de localiser dans l'Extrême-Orient.

Sans médiation, la guerre peut se prolonger indéfiniment. La Russie, qui ne peut être atteinte par le Japon dans ses possessions européennes, sera retenue de demander la paix par son amour-propre national, alors même que son véritable intérêt serait de mettre fin à une guerre qui la ruine. De son côté, le Japon, après ses premiers succès, s'abstiendra de renouveler spontanément des conditions modérées et raisonnables, alors cependant qu'une prolongation indéfinie de la guerre le conduira à une banqueroute qui serait la fin de ses légitimes ambitions.

Le moment est donc favorable et la médiation urgente. C'est pourquoi je demanderai à l'assemblée de supprimer dans le texte qui lui est soumis, les mots "au moment opportun." Si nous avons l'air d'admettre que le moment actuel puisse n'être pas opportun, il est à craindre que nous ne justifiions tous les atermoiements. Tous, ici, nous sommes convaincus de l'urgence et dès lors nous ferions mieux de le dire. Les mots dont je demande la suppression ne figuraient pas d'ailleurs dans le texte original de la proposition, telle que je l'ai soumise au conseil de l'Union interparlementaire.

Un autre amendement que je voudrais introduire consiste à intercaler les mots "soit individuellement, soit collectivement." Si nous devons attendre une intervention collective des puissances, nous risquons d'attendre longtemps. Une initiative isolée serait parfaitement en situation, et à cet égard, qu'il me soit permis de dire, en mon nom personnel et sans vouloir engager la Conférence, combien il serait souhaitable de voir cette initiative prise par le Président de la grande République Américaine, qui a déjà rendu tant de services à la cause de l'arbitrage et de la paix.

Assurément, notre Conférence a le droit de voter la résolution qui lui est soumise. Nous ne sommes pas ici une simple assemblée de pacifistes qui se bornent à faire des discours. Nous constituons une réunion de groupes investis chacun d'une part de l'autorité gouvernementale, exerçant chacun une influence plus ou moins considérable sur la direction des affaires publiques, dans nos Etats respectifs. Cette situation nous impose une certaine réserve, mais elle nous impose aussi l'impérieux devoir d'élever la voix quand nous croyons pouvoir favoriser la cause de la paix par une recommandation pratique. Agir autrement, ce serait supprimer notre utilité et notre raison d'être. Si nous devions nous borner à nous réunir, tantôt dans un pays, tantôt dans un autre, pour profiter d'une généreuse et splendide hospitalité, comme celle que nous offre aujourd'hui le gouvernement américain, je n'hésite pas à dire que nous resterions au-dessous de notre mission et de notre idéal.

La Convention de La Haye a formellement reconnu que des tiers pouvaient, en toutes circonstances, soit avant, soit pendant la guerre, offrir leurs bons offices dans l'intérêt de la paix, sans que les belligérants puissent s'en offenser, et aussi sans que le rejet de cette médiation pût être regardé comme une offense. Je n'ai pas besoin d'ajouter que le vœu soumis à vos délibérations n'implique aucune pensée hostile aux puissances en cause. C'est pour la Russie un moyen honorable de se tirer d'une situation difficile. Quant au Japon, il s'est montré jusqu'ici très soucieux d'entrer dans la communion des puissances civilisées. Il en a certainement le droit, et il ne pourrait trouver une meilleure occasion de le faire reconnaître par les puissances neutres. Personnellement, j'estime que l'existence d'un empire fort et éclairé au Japon peut devenir une garantie de l'équilibre international; toutefois, c'est sous la réserve que cet empire soit, non un fauteur de guerre et de haines raciales, mais un élément de civilisation et de paix.

M. La Fontaine, sénateur de Belgique, propose à la seconde partie de la première phrase de la résolution un amendement ainsi conçu: "regrettant que les puissances signataires des conventions de La Haye, lors de l'ouverture des hostilités, ne soient pas intervenues plus énergiquement et n'aient pas offert leur médiation aux termes des conventions susvisées."

MM. Paul Strauss, sénateur français, et di San Giuliano repoussent cet amendement, estimant qu'il contient un blâme à l'égard des puissances.

M. Gobat l'appuie, en alléguant que les puissances ayant, aux termes de la convention de La Haye du 29 juillet 1899, le devoir d'offrir leurs bons offices dans le cas où un conflit menace d'éclater entre une ou plusieurs puissances contractantes, l'amendement de M. La Fontaine ne dépasse ni dans son texte, ni dans son esprit, la portée de cette convention.

M. Goblet d'Alviella propose deux amendements: supprimer au deuxième alinéa les mots: "au moment opportun" et intercaler à la place ceux-ci: "collectivement ou individuellement."

M. Forgemol de Bostquenard, sénateur français, propose d'ajouter le mot "amicalement" après "d'intervenir."

M. Gobat. C'est bien ainsi que l'intervention doit être comprise et cela va de soi.

Personne ne demandant plus la parole, il est procédé au vote.

Les amendements proposés par M. Goblet d'Alviella sont acceptés, le premier par 36 voix centre 31, le second à l'unanimité.

Celui de M. La Fontaine est rejeté par 34 voix contre 28.

Enfin l'assemblée accepte à l'unanimité la résolution dans les termes suivants:

La Conférence interparlementaire, émue par les horreurs de la guerre qui se poursuit en Extrême-Orient entre deux Etats civilisés, et regrettant que des puissances signataires des conventions de La Haye n'aient pu avoir recours aux clauses qui les invitent à offrir leur médiation dès l'ouverture des hostilités,

Prie les puissances signataires de La Haye d'intervenir, collectivement ou individuellement, auprès des belligérants, pour faciliter le rétablissement de la paix, et charge le Bureau interparlementaire de porter la présente résolution à la connaissance des dites puissances.

Le Président met ensuite en délibération le No. 5 de l'ordre du jour: Invitation aux puissances de convoquer une deuxième session de la Conférence de La Haye.

M. Burton (Etats-Unis). I congratulate you upon this auspicious occasion. A cause is fortunate when its object is in harmony with the trend of events and its advocates may have an assured confidence in its ultimate success. Such certainly is true of the desire to substitute peaceful means for bloodshed in the settlement of international disputes. It is no visionary purpose to seek to decide questions between nations in the same way as those between individuals, but a practical aim, based on reason and humanity. If we consider the history of the past hundred years, there has been an increasing tendency in this direction. The most notable date was that which marked the close of the Napoleonic wars in the year 1815, a date almost as important as the end of the so-called Dark Ages. Prior to that time the most advanced nations of Europe had been engaged in almost constant war, but then, softened by calamity and exhausted by the strain of years of struggle, a more peaceful disposition prevailed. It began to be considered that the sovereign existed for the benefit of the people rather than the people for the aggrandizement of the sovereign. The individual became more and the nation less. No country could engage in war on slight occasion. Alliances between nations were based upon a desire to maintain peace and prevent a disturbance in the balance of power. At about this time religious wars between different branches of the Christian church ceased and controversies of a religious nature were followed by war only between Christian and Mohammedan, and these for the most part were confined to contests arising from racial or religious differences in the Balkan Peninsula.

In numerous instances the fruits of conquest have been denied to the victor, so that he has been allowed to annex but a small portion of the territory of the vanquished. In the acquisition of unexplored territory or that which belongs to uncivilized nations and tribes, spheres of influence have been defined with great care, so that a clash may be avoided between contending civilized nations. What has been the result? The comforts and advantages of life have multiplied in less than a hundred years more than in all the ages preceding. Inventions of the preceding century began to be utilized when peace was declared. Then came the development of the steamboat, the beginnings of the railway, and later the marvelous achievements of electricity. Man has gained, year by year, a new power over nature, and all these advances, year by year, have inured to the benefit of all mankind. These advantages will continue and will still further multiply if there can be banished from the history of nations the preparation for war and the thought that national controversies must be settled upon the field of battle.

The last year has been most notable in the number of arbitration treaties. The new century was not ushered in merely by the blowing of whistles and the burning of bonfires, but by the quiet and unobtrusive triumphs of peace. Since October 1, 1903, numerous arbitration treaties have been concluded or acted upon, such as that of England with France, and each of these countries with Italy and Spain. True, these treaties contain a limitation to the effect that the questions at issue shall not affect the vital interests, the independence, or the honor of the two contracting States, but more important than their phraseology is the tendency which they manifest. Already in pursuance of this treaty between them a convention has been entered into between France and England by which controversies of a century's standing are to be settled amicably. Most progressive of all these treaties is the one between Denmark and the Netherlands mentioned yesterday by the honorable gentlemen from those two nations. This absolutely has no limitation. It insures perpetual peace between these countries, and yet no one can claim that the people of Holland or Denmark are lacking in vigor or in courage. The foremost capital of the world in the centuries past has been at the mercy of the fleets or sailors of each of these countries. Their influence extends through all the earth, and never with more beneficent effect than in the lesson of the recent treaty enacted between them. The list of arbitration treaties negotiated within six months included half a dozen last April. It would now be necessary to add several others to the list.

In the eighty-nine years since 1815, more than 200 threatening and troublesome controversies between nations have been settled by arbitration. This method of avoiding war has been chosen not merely by countries of Europe and North and South America but has been adopted as well by those of Asia and Africa, such as Persia, Afghanistan, Siam, and China; also by Egypt and the Transvaal Republic. By a singular coincidence in figures, the United States was a párty in 50 of the first 100 of these, and in 25 of the second 100, thus proving a measure of leadership, and also the more frequent adoption of this method by other nations later. I say this in no boastful spirit. We are proud of our country here and everywhere, but the individual or nation is insignificant in a cause such as that which we advocate to-day.

As citizens of the United States, we must recognize that our marvelous growth has been coincident with a great world movement, not confined to one country or to one continent, during which the swelling tides of progress have been rising higher and higher. Just as a State of the United States enjoys great opportunities because it is one of a union of States, so any nation enjoys great possibilities because it is one of a family of nations.

The resolution presented respectfully and cordially requests the President of the United States to invite all the nations to send representatives to a conference which shall further consider and, if possible, conclude the work commenced at The Hague Conference. It is due to this organization to say that the general proposals considered and enacted at The Hague Conference were considered at an earlier time at its meetings, and are in the same line with reports made to this body at its meetings prior to 1899. In framing the resolution it was thought desirable to take up the work where it was left by The Hague Conference. Great benefits have already resulted from that gathering. It has furnished a tribunal for the settlement of international disputes and was also effective in securing agreements which must greatly diminish the horrors of war on land and on sea. It would seem best that this tribunal be resorted to as far as possible, so that the different Governments of the world may realize that there is a prompt and satisfactory means available for settling disputes, and that the prestige of the court and the sanction afforded to its decisions may be increased year by year. The committee presenting the resolution thought best to include in one paragraph all questions left unfinished at The Hague Conference. Different members of this Interparliamentary Union may ascribe unequal degrees of importance to these questions. It should, however, be said that the proposition for the arrest or limitation of military and naval armaments is one which is bound to assume exceptional prominence. The burdens of armed peace are becoming almost intolerable. On this subject M. Block has said, in detailing the expense and difficulty of the present situation: "Such are the consequences of the so-called armed peace of Europe—slow destruction in consequence of expenditures on preparation for war or swift destruction in the event of war; in both events convulsions in the social order." It should also be said that the constant temptation to employ these great military and naval armaments is an ever-present menace to the world's peace.

Other questions left over are the rights and duties of neutrals, the quality of arms to be used in naval warfare, the inviolability of private property on the sea, and the question of the bombardment of ports by a naval force. Some of these questions are included in the scope of other resolutions to be presented to-day.

A conference called in accordance with the resolution presented, it is hoped, will lend to the negotiation of arbitration treaties between the nations represented. The resolution also provides that there shall be considered the advisability of establishing an international congress to convene periodically for the discussion of international questions. These questions are assuming so great importance that the cause of peace will be greatly promoted by a full and free discussion of the principles of international law and the means to secure amity among nations. In no way can these objects be more efficiently promoted than by an international congress made up of representatives or delegates from the civilized nations of the earth.

M. le comte APPONYI appuie chaleureusement la résolution.

M. GOBAT. Je considère la résolution dont il s'agit comme la plus importante de notre ordre du jour. D'une part il est nécessaire, la Conférence de La Haye de 1899 ayant prévu qu'il y en aurait d'ultérieures, de ne pas laisser tomber en désuétude l'importante, l'indispensable institution des Congrès généraux des Etats. Il faut, d'autre part, que ces Conférences soient organisées et qu'elles deviennent périodiques. En leur donnant une organisation, on verra combien il sera facile de créer un nouveau rouage dans les ententes générales qui ont été ébauchées à La Haye. Pourquoi, par exemple, ne conférerait-on pas à une délégation de la prochaine Conférence le soin de préparer la suivante, de veiller à l'exécution de ses décisions comme aussi à la loyale application des traités internationaux? Ce serait le très précieux quoique modeste début d'une organisation politique semblable à celle des Etats-Unis. L'Union interparlementaire doit en tous cas viser avant toutes choses, maintenant que les traités d'arbitrage sont acceptés par toutes les puissances, à ce que cette organisation politique soit mise à l'ordre du jour des puissances et elle a le devoir d'en faire, dès à présent, l'objet principal de ses propres aspirations. J'appuie donc de toutes mes forces la résolution et je demande que la Conférence interparlementaire de Saint Louis aille, *in corpore*, la présenter à M. le Président Roosevelt à Washington.

M. CLARKE (Grande-Bretagne) propose de supprimer la proposition sous lettre *c* de la résolution.

MM. STANHOPE et DI SAN GIULIANO s'y opposent et M. Clarke se déclare satisfait.

Le résolution est ensuite acceptée à l'unanimité dans les termes suivants:

Considérant que l'opinion publique éclairée et l'esprit de la civilisation moderne exigent que les différends entre nations soient réglés de la même manière que les contestations entre individus, c'est-à-dire par des cours de justice et conformément à des principes légaux reconnus,

La conférence demande que les divers gouvernements du monde entier délèguent des représentants à une conférence internationale, qui devra se réunir à l'époque et au lieu désignés par eux, pour délibérer sur les questions suivantes, savoir:

(*a*) les points ajournés par la Conférence de La Haye,

(*b*) la négociation de traités d'arbitrage entre les nations qui seront représentées à cette conférence,

(*c*) l'opportunité de créer un Congrès international qui se réunirait périodiquement pour discuter les questions internationales,

Et décide de prier respectueusement le Président des Etats Unis d'inviter toutes les nations à se faire représenter à cette conférence.

LE PRÉSIDENT met en délibération le No. 6 de l'ordre du jour: question des mines et autres explosifs sous-marins.

M. le comte APPONYI expose que la proposition émane de son collègue Pazmandy, que celui-ci devait être rapporteur et qu'il n'est pas préparé pour le remplacer. M. Snape a offert d'exposer la question.

M. SNAPE (Grande-Bretagne) recommande l'adoption de la résolution présentée par le Conseil interparlementaire, appuyant surtout sur les dangers que les mines sous-marines font courir aux neutres. Il cite le cas de mines posées pendant une guerre, qui ont fait explosion après la fin des hostilités et détruit un navire de commerce.

M. BRUNIALTI, sénateur italien, combat la proposition. Les explosifs sous-marins sont indispensables à la défense des côtes et des mers.

De même MM. PIRIE et BRYN-ROBERTS (Grande-Bretagne).

M. La Fontaine pose la question préalable.

En considération de cette opposition et pour ne pas entamer la valeur morale de la résolution proposée, M. le comte Apponyi déclare retirer la proposition.

Le Président annonce que la troisième et dernière séance aura lieu au Southern Hotel, à 9 heures du matin.

La séance est levée à 1 heure 30.

SÉANCE DE MERCREDI, 14 SEPTEMBRE 1904, AU SOUTHERN HOTEL.

Le Président, après avoir communiqué à l'assemblée plusieurs invitations adressées aux membres de la Conférence, donne lecture du télégramme suivant:

Nobel Committee of Norwegian Parliament salutes first conference in United States whose President and statesmen have so successfully promoted international arbitration.

(Signed)   Loveland, *President.*

et met en délibération le No. 4 de l'ordre du jour.

M. Gobat. La résolution qui vous est soumise au sujet du progrès remarquable des idées pacifiques, a été formulée par M. de Plener, le distingué président de la Conférence de Vienne, et devait vous être exposée par lui. Empêché de se rendre en Amérique, il m'a prié de le remplacer. Je le fais d'autant plus volontiers que ma tâche consiste à constater des événements dont les membres de l'Union interparlementaire ont particulièrement lieu de se féliciter. Je veux parler des nombreux traités d'arbitrage conclus depuis notre dernière Conférence. Il y en a dix; quelques-uns sont énumérés dans le projet de résolution qui vous est soumis. A vrai dire, si l'on ne considérait que la clause arbitrale, telle qu'elle se trouve insérée dans ces traités, nous ne pourrions témoigner un grand enthousiasme. La plupart admettent une formule très étroite réservant les intérêts vitaux, l'indépendance et l'honneur des Etats, trois idées plutôt vagues, sur lesquelles les opinions peuvent varier. Au moyen de cette réserve, les parties contractantes pourraient aisément, un conflit venant à surgir, se soustraire à l'engagement de le soumettre à des arbitres. Mais n'oublions pas que l'Europe s'est montrée généralement rebelle envers le principe de l'arbitrage international, qu'un appel adressé, il y a une vingtaine d'années, par les Etats-Unis à l'Ancien Monde, y a rencontré peu d'écho.

Quelque imparfaits que soient les traités dont il s'agit, nous saluons en eux une initiative, un commencement, un début, l'éclosion du sentiment de la justice et de la solidarité humaine, l'acheminement dans le domaine pratique de théories fondamentales aussi vieilles que le monde, mais combien jeunes et nouvelles dans la réalité des choses. Il est désormais acquis que les nations ne veulent plus se ruer les unes sur les autres pour régler leurs difficultés; elles font des réserves pour la forme seulement afin de sacrifier encore à la routine et aux futiles usages diplomatiques. Mais qu'importeront ces réserves, lorsque deux puissances, unies malgré tout par un contrat, seront obligées de discuter s'il s'agit d'intérêts vitaux, d'honneur ou d'indépendance? Deux adversaires, obligés de causer ensemble avant de se battre, sont bien près de s'entendre. Il est regrettable néanmoins que ces conventions ne soient pas nettes comme celle conclue entre le Danemark et les Pays-Bas qui ne contient aucune réserve, qui est l'arbitrage sans phrase. Respect aux gouvernements de ces deux pays.

On a signé autres choses que des traités d'arbitrage. Les arrangements franco-britanniques sont une manifestation plus importante encore. La France et l'Angleterre ont mis fin, par une entente, à plusieurs conflits très anciens qui altéraient la cordialité de leurs relations et pouvaient un jour ou l'autre occasionner de graves complications. C'est le procédé le plus recommandable qu'il y ait, et la meilleure garantie de la paix. Puissent d'autres gouvernements suivre le bel exemple que l'Angleterre et la France ont donné au monde.

Il est permis de tirer une conséquence pratique des traités d'arbitrage signés entre les Etats et de leurs autres arrangements; du moment que la plupart des puissances s'engagent à soumettre leurs différends à l'arbitrage, elles doivent, si elles sont sincères, s'entendre pour réduire leurs armements. C'est une loi que la logique leur impose.

Je vous recommande la résolution proposée par le Conseil interparlementaire.

M. CLARKE demande que le traité d'arbitrage conclu entre le Danemark et les Pays-Bas, le plus remarquable de tous, soit aussi mentionné dans la résolution.

M. W. RANDAL CREMER, membre de la Chambre des communes, propose que tous les traités d'arbitrage y soient énumérés.

M. EMILE TIBBAUT, député belge. Il serait peut-être difficile pour l'assemblée de faire une énumération exacte de tous les pays qui ont conclu des traités d'arbitrage au cours de cette dernière période. Ainsi je crois, sans pouvoir l'affirmer, que la Belgique est de ce nombre. Pour éviter des erreurs qui seraient regrettables, ne serait-il pas plus prudent de laisser à Monsieur le secrétaire le soin de faire cette énumération dans une note ou un renvoi. L'énumération ne ferait pas partie du corps de notre résolution; elle ne serait qu'un renseignement complémentaire; de la sorte, l'assemblée échapperait au danger d'être inexacte ou incomplète.

M. BRDLIK, membre du Reichsrat autrichien. Voulez-vous permettre au représentant d'une nation certes pas bien grande, mais, à mon avis, très intelligente, d'exprimer sa vive satisfaction au sujet du développement des idées pacifiques et de vous prier d'accueillir avec bienveillance la résolution que le rapporteur, M. Gobat, vient de nous présenter. Je vous adresse cette prière, non seulement au nom de ma propre nation, mais aussi au nom de toutes les autres nations slaves habitant l'Autriche. La nation tchèque, à laquelle j'appartiens, désire la paix, sachant très bien que les fruits du travail national ne peuvent se développer qu'en temps de paix et que précisément par un labeur assidu la nation tchèque, ainsi que toutes les autres nations, arriveront à leur désir commun, à la liberté et l'indépendance. C'est une chose bien connue que les petites nations ne récoltent rien des guerres et qu'elles risquent tout au plus d'être opprimées ou menacées dans leur existence.

Le peuple tchèque, que j'ai l'honneur de représenter dans cette assemblée, et dont j'ai toujours défendu les intérêts moraux et politiques, non seulement au Parlement, mais partout où l'occasion s'en présentait, considère comme son droit le devoir sacré de combattre pour la liberté. Cette lutte acharnée pour conquérir son indépendance politique et nationale, il la continuera au vingtième siècle, ère du prétendu progrès.

Voilà pourquoi la nation tchèque, ainsi que toutes les autres nations slaves habitant l'Autriche, s'allieront toujours à celles qui poursuivent le même but et qui luttent pour la liberté et l'anoblissement de l'humanité.

Mais comme tous ces nobles efforts ne peuvent réussir que sous les auspices de la paix, je souhaite, Messieurs, de tout mon cœur, au nom du peuple tchèque, un succès complet aux nobles travaux que vous entreprenez pour l'avancement de la concorde entre les nations et de la liberté.

MM. Howard Vincent et Lough, membres de la Chambre des Communes, appuient M. Cremer.

La proposition de ce dernier est acceptée.

En conséquence, l'assemblée vote la résolution dans les termes suivants:

"La conférence exprime sa vive satisfaction au sujet du développement des idées pacifiques pendant l'année dernière, notamment de la conclusion de traités d'arbitrage entre la France et la Grande-Bretagne, la France et l'Italie, la France et l'Espagne, la France et les Pays-Bas, la Grande-Bretagne et l'Italie, la Grande-Bretagne et l'Espagne, la Grande-Bretagne et l'Allemagne, la Grande-Bretagne et la Suède et la Norvège, le Danemark et les Pays-Bas, l'Espagne et le Portugal, qui doivent être suivis de conventions d'arbitrage entre d'autres Etats; elle voit dans les accords récemment conclus entre la France et la Grande-Bretagne pour l'arrangement des questions coloniales qui étaient litigieuses depuis longtemps entre ces deux puissances, un événement heureux et important, et invite les autres gouvernements à procéder de la même manière, en supprimant, si faire se peut, d'un commun accord, des différends invétérés qui pourraient amener un jour de graves complications, s'ils n'étaient arrangés à temps par une entente mutuelle.

Le Président met en délibération le No. 7 de l'ordre du jour.

M. Snape rapporte au lieu de M. Hepburn. Après différentes observations concernant l'opportunité de traiter un objet qui a déjà été discuté par la Conférence de Berne, la proposition est retirée.

Le Président met en délibération le No. 8 de l'ordre du jour.

M. Gobat, rapporteur. Je me bornerai à quelques observations, les termes de la résolution qui vous est proposée étant suffisamment explicites. Il s'agit de savoir de quelle manière et par quel moyens l'action de l'Union interparlementaire pourrait être renforcée. J'ai toujours considéré une forte organisation des groupes interparlementaires comme la condition principale d'une forte organisation de l'Union elle-même. Dans les pays où les groupes ne sont pas constitués, où ils ne se réunissent jamais, où ils ne s'occupent pas même dans leurs Parlements des questions qui devraient intéresser en tout premier lieu leurs membres, les groupes n'existent pas en réalité. Il est vraiment surprenant que dans les corps législatifs, où une foule d'affaires se traitent préalablement dans des sections, comme les questions agricoles, ouvrières, sociales et autres, il n'y ait pas un groupe qui s'occupe spécialement des affaires internationales, les plus importantes de toutes au point de vue de la paix universelle et de la justice. Cela regarde la diplomatie, dit-on. Soit, puisque diplomates il y a; mais cela regarde encore beaucoup plus le pays et ses représentants. On laisse jouer, dans la plupart des Etats, à la diplomatie, un rôle qu'elle ne devrait pas jouer, qu'elle ne joue ni aux Etats-Unis, ni en Suisse; on lui abandonne pour ainsi dire comme un monopole les relations étrangères et le soin d'arranger celles-ci de telle manière qu'elles doivent un jour ou l'autre amener des complications.

Ceux qui prétendent se désintéresser des affaires internationales ne devraient cependant pas oublier que la guerre franco-allemande et la guerre russo-japonaise sont l'œuvre de la diplomatie. Que les députés et sénateurs partisans de la justice entre les nations s'organisent donc, pour être en mesure d'intervenir dans les discussions parlementaires ou de prendre des initiatives chaque fois que les intérêts de la légalité internationale seront en jeu. Il est désirable bien entendu que, vu la haute importance de ces intérêts, les groupes interparlementaires se forment de membres appartenant à toutes les fractions politiques, et que devant la grandeur de la tâche les rivalités des partis s'effacent. Les groupes devraient aussi être tenus au courant et tenir leurs Parlements, dans la langue du pays, au courant de tout ce qui se passe dans l'Union. Pour toutes les grandes communautés embrassant plusieurs pays, la diversité du langage est un obstacle; mais on peut aisément le surmonter. Plusieurs groupes distribuent à leurs membres ainsi qu'aux Parlements des traductions des communications du Bureau interparlementaire et des décisions de nos conférences.

Le point faible de l'Union est l'organisation insuffisante du Bureau interparlementaire. D'une part celui-ci manque de renseignements parce que la constitution des groupes étant défectueuse ou faisant défaut, personne ne l'informe d'une quantité de choses qu'il devrait savoir; d'autre part, les minimes ressources mises à la disposition du

Bureau ne permettent pas à celui qui le dirige de lui consacrer tout son temps et toutes ses forces. Nous sommes encore dans le provisoire; on a créé le Bureau en 1892, afin que l'existence de la Conférence interparlementaire soit manifestée au moyen d'une enseigne; on lui a tracé un programme; on attend de lui de grandes choses, des initiatives, des interventions; mais on ne le met pas en mesure de les accomplir, de sorte qu'il est forcément réduit à gérer les affaires courantes.

L'avenir de l'Union interparlementaire est donc une question d'argent. On prétend que notre institution obtiendra des dons, lorsqu'elle sera constituée en corporation publiquement reconnue. Je ferai les démarches nécessaires, si vous acceptez la résolution qui vous est soumise, afin que d'une manière ou de l'autre l'Union interparlementaire ou le Bureau obtiennent en Suisse la personnalité juridique. Enfin il serait très utile, sinon indispensable, que l'Union ait un organe officiel. Elle en a eu un pendant trois ans, mais ne l'a pas suffisamment soutenu. On pourrait peut-être désigner " L'Indépendance Belge " comme notre organe; c'est la feuille qui s'occupe le plus du mouvement pacifique.

MM. Stanhope et le comte **Apponyi** appuient les conclusions de la résolution, ce dernier en faisant des réserves au sujet du journal.

M. Tibbaut, député belge. Je remercie le comte Apponyi d'avoir signalé l'inconvénient du choix d'un journal. Pour qu'un journal puisse être l'organe de l'Union interparlementaire, il faudrait, comme condition essentielle, qu'il se meuve dans la sphère élevée du droit international et qu'il n'ait aucun rapport avec la politique des pays affiliés à la Ligue. Or, cela n'est pas le cas pour le journal proposé. Je n'ai au surplus qu'à me rallier, sur ce point, aux considérations qu'a fait valoir M. le comte Apponyi.

Mais, Messieurs, je vais plus loin; et j'ajoute qu'il serait dangereux, nuisible à notre cause, d'avoir un organe permanent de la Ligue, même s'il est limité aux seules questions du droit international.

Notre Union n'a qu'une force morale, et cette force doit être gardée intacte. Elle se manifeste surtout lorsque, à la suite de faits précis, comme dans le cas de la guerre russo-japonaise, l'Union émet en assemblée générale des vœux qui ont été délibérés en commun et qui apparaissent alors comme l'expression des sentiments des peuples et des nations. Ce sont là des manifestations solennelles, dont le caractère sérieux et grave ne saurait être mis en doute.

Je craindrais d'affaiblir l'importance de notre Union et de nos décisions, si elle créait un journal de propagande. Quel peut être l'effet d'un article écrit par une ou plusieurs personnes, sans délibération préalable de l'Union réunie en assemblée générale ou représentée par son Bureau? N'est-ce pas parce que le journal contient généralement l'expression hâtive et personnelle, que le journalisme a une puissance relativement faible dans le milieu intellectuel? Et si l'on prétendait faire passer pour une doctrine acceptée par l'Union les articles que les membres n'ont pas eu l'occasion d'examiner et de discuter, ne s'exposerait-on pas à des erreurs, à des discussions et à des demandes? Ne s'expose-t-on pas à donner ainsi le spectacle de la désunion? Quant à moi, j'ai pour habitude de n'accepter que ce que j'ai été mis en état d'approuver, soit par la discussion, soit par ma signature.

Quel pourrait être d'ailleurs le but de cette propagande? S'adresserait-elle au public? Mais le peuple n'a pas besoin de cette propagande; le désir de la paix, il le porte dans ses entrailles. S'adresserait-elle aux membres de l'Union? Mais, nous tous, nous sommes les partisans convaincus de la paix, et c'est pour ce motif que nous nous réunissons et que nous faisons ces démarches solennelles auxquelles la discussion préalable donne tant d'importance. Sur les faits tels que la guerre russo-japonaise, nous ne risquons pas de nous diviser, et c'est à l'unanimité que nous prenons nos décisions, alors que nous serions bien près de nous diviser s'il fallait s'engager sur le terrain de la théorie.

La propagande s'adresse-t-elle aux gouvernements? Ce serait de l'illusion que de le croire; car je le répète, notre force est purement morale; et elle peut être grande si elle émane d'une assemblée composée des délégués de toutes les nations et se prononçant avec unanimité après un sérieux examen.

L'exposé d'idées personnelles ou d'idées appartenant à un nombre restreint de rédacteurs, quelle que soit la valeur personnelle des rédacteurs, ne saurait rien apporter au prestige de notre Union; au contraire, il risquerait de le diminuer par des polémiques et des discussions qui nuiraient peut-être même à la force morale des délibérations de nos assemblées.

Au fond de la proposition faite par le Bureau et développée par M. Gobat, il y a une idée juste. Il est à désirer qu'il y ait des membres dont la mission spéciale serait de suivre et d'étudier le mouvement de la paix internationale et de communiquer aux membres de l'Union tous les renseignements utiles. Mais à cet effet il ne faut pas de journal. Une communication par bulletin spécial suffit. Chaque membre pourrait, s'il le juge utile, le transmettre aux journaux importants de son pays. De la sorte, non seulement les membres seraient tenus au courant, mais la publicité se ferait large et efficace par tous les organes de la presse des pays affiliés.

Ce mode de travailler nous mettrait à l'abri des polémiques qui porteraient atteinte à la force morale nécessaire pour l'obtention de résultats sérieux. Si des événements se produisent qui nécessitent des décisions urgentes, le Bureau est tout indiqué pour prendre la place de l'Union et agir en son nom; il dispose à cet effet de toute notre confiance et son action réunit toutes les garanties d'une autorité consciente de son devoir et de sa haute mission.

M. Lund insiste sur la nécessité de procurer au Bureau interparlementaire les moyens de travailler.

M. Gniewosz reconnaît que la conservation de l'Union interparlementaire est due au Bureau et regrette que l'on ne s'occupe pas plus sérieusement de lui assurer une dotation convenable.

MM. Houzeau, Byles (Grande-Bretagne), Tydeman, Madison (Grande-Bretagne), Hellepütte (Belgique), Clarke et Lough prennent la parole sur la question du journal. Les uns proposent de choisir un organe dans la presse qui appuie les tendances pacifistes; les autres de publier un bulletin périodique sommaire.

M. Grant, député à la Chambre des Communes, propose de supprimer la conclusion concernant le journal.

M. Ernst Beckman. Chargé par le groupe suédois de proposer un amendement à nos statuts, je pense que c'est maintenant le moment de le faire en proposant une addition à la résolution que nous allons voter. Le rapporteur, M. Gobat, et le conseil m'ont déjà déclaré leur adhésion. La chose étant très simple, mais néanmoins d'une certaine importance pour le développement de notre Union, je ne pense pas qu'elle puisse soulever des objections. Depuis longtemps le groupe suédois sent le besoin de profiter des expériences des autres groupes parlementaires. Mais, comment s'y prendre. Autant que je sache, il y a peu de groupes qui publient des comptes rendus. Comment donc se renseigner sur leur organisation, leur œuvre, leur manière de faire la propagande? Evidemment des comptes rendus réguliers favoriseraient d'une manière aussi simple qu'efficace l'action de l'Union. Ce serait un moyen des meilleurs pour créer des rapports plus intimes entre les groupes nationaux. Ils serviraient sans aucun doute à stimuler l'action de ces groupes et ainsi à renforcer notre Union. Mon ami, M. Edouard Wavrinsky, dont je regrette beaucoup l'absence, a déjà proposé, dans la séance du Conseil à Bruxelles cette année, que chaque groupe soit tenu de remettre au Bureau interparlementaire, avant le mois de mars, un compte rendu de ces travaux pendant l'année, et qu'un résumé de ces comptes rendus soit remis avant la fin du mois de septembre, au plus tard, en nombre suffisant d'exemplaires aux bureaux des groupes nationaux. C'est pour cette proposition que je demande votre adhésion, en laissant au Bureau interparlementaire le soin de formuler l'amendement nécessaire aux statuts.

M. Delbet, député français, dépose sur le bureau une proposition de M. Dauron qui lui paraît rentrer dans le sujet en discussion; elle a trait à l'organisation d'une fête internationale annuelle de la paix.

M. Gobat. J'accepte la proposition de M. Beckman à titre de motion concernant la revision des statuts; il y sera donné suite, cas échéant, à la prochaine Conférence. Quant à la communication de M. Delbet, elle doit être renvoyée au conseil.

La discussion étant épuisée, il est procédé au vote.

23306—05——7

La proposition de M. Grant obtient la majorité; les motions de MM. Beckman et Delbet sont renvoyées au conseil et la résolution est acceptée dans les termes suivants:

Dans le but de renforcer l'action de l'Union interparlementaire, il est désirable:

(*a*) Que les groupes interparlementaires aient une forte organisation, qu'ils s'occupent spécialement des questions internationales et qu'il concertent des actions preparatoires ou décisives dans leurs parlements;

(*b*) Qu'il soit reconnu que les membres des groupes interparlementaires sont, en vue des actions concertées, solidaires, sans distinction des fractions politiques auxquelles ils peuvent appartenir;

(*c*) Que les groupes interparlementaires répandent dans leurs parlements, traduites dans la langue du pays, toutes les communications qui leur seront faites par les organes de l'Union interparlementaire;

(*d*) Que le Bureau interparlementaire soit organisé de telle sorte qu'il puisse centraliser et coordonner tous les documents relatifs aux affaires diplomatiques et en communiquer des extraits utiles quand il le jugera nécessaire;

(*e*) Que le Bureau interparlementaire soit constitué en personne juridique.

Le Conseil interparlementaire est invité à exécuter immédiatement cette dernière résolution et pour le surplus, en tant que besoin, à soumettre des propositions à la prochaine conférence.

Le président donne la parole à M. Gobat, pour son rapport.

M. GOBAT. Une année s'est écoulée depuis la Conférence de Vienne. Je constate que cette assemblée, de toutes celles tenues jusqu'à ce jour, a joui de la plus grande notoriété. D'un bout à l'autre de l'Europe, la presse s'en est occupée et a publié des comptes rendus, accompagnés généralement de commentaires sympathiques. Les journaux de la capitale de l'Autriche, organes d'une population sincèrement attachée aux aspirations pacifiques, s'étant appliqués, avec un zèle remarquable, dont nous les remercions, à donner aux délibérations de la XIIe Conference une publicité étendue, la presse des autres pays a suivi son exemple. Je note ce résultat réjouissant pour établir combien il importe d'intéresser les gazettes du siège des Conférences interparlementaires aux travaux de celle-ci. Si nous n'avons pas encore pu engager la presse dans une coopération directe à nos efforts, sachons tout au moins profiter, pour nos assemblées générales, des puissants moyens d'action dont elle dispose. Elle est un auxiliaire dont nous avons absolument besoin.

Le Bureau de l'Union interparlementaire a exécuté les décisions de la Conférence de Vienne, en communiquant à qui de droit les décisions de celle-ci. J'ai ensuite collaboré à la rédaction du compte rendu de cette assemblée. Le comité autrichien eut l'excellente idée de renouveler le recensement des membres de l'Union, que j'ai fait, il y a une dizaine d'années, dans notre défunte revue "La Conférence interparlementaire." Ce recensement accuse un nombre de plus de 2,000 membres, non compris les Etats-Unis, dont le groupe n'était pas encore formé. Quelle force ce chiffre représente, et quelle force bien plus grande il représenterait si elle était mieux organisée.

Le Bureau international de la paix nous ayant demandé de communiquer aux groupes de l'Union les résolutions du XIIe Congrès universel de la Paix, tenu à Rouen, concernant l'arrêt des armements, le droit de la paix et l'aérostation militaire, j'accédai à ce désir, en faisant cette communication aux membres du conseil.

J'ai essayé de fonder un groupe de l'Union en Grèce, le seul des pays européens gouvernés constitutionnellement, qui ne fasse pas partie de cette institution. M'étant procuré les adresses de quelques députés influents, je leur fis des ouvertures en leurs envoyant nos comptes rendus, ainsi que les publications du Bureau et leur demandai d'organiser un groupe. L'un d'eux me répondit qu'il le ferait. Mais jusqu'ici sa promesse n'a pas été réalisée. L'agitation qui règne dans les Balkans explique jusqu'à un certain point cette circonstance.

Au surplus, l'administrateur du Bureau interparlementaire, en dehors du travail courant très considérable qui lui incombe—sa correspondance seule comprend trois cent quatre-vingt quatre lettres et huit circulaires, depuis la Conférence de Vienne—a été très absorbé par l'organisation de la conférence de Saint Louis.

Cette cité avait été désignée conditionnellement comme siège de notre douzième assemblée générale. Il était entendu que l'invitation personnelle du délégué américain à la Conférence de Vienne serait confirmée par celle d'un groupe interparlementaire. Rentré dans ses foyers, M. Bartholdt put assez rapidement fonder un groupe qui ratifia son invitation, ce que je m'empressai de communiquer aux membres du Conseil interparlementaire. Puis, notre honorable collègue des Etats-Unis déposa à la Chambre des représentants du Congrès un projet de résolution, aux termes duquel le Congrès lui-même devait, à son tour, adresser une invitation aux membres de l'Union interparlementaire. Dans l'intervalle je reçus celle du groupe américain, motivée et formulée dans toutes les règles. J'en fis immédiatement communication au Conseil interparlementaire. Puis vint la décision du Congrès lui-même; invitation cordiale adressée à l'Union interparlementaire de tenir nos assemblées générales dans une ville des Etats-Unis, avec allocation nécessaire pour couvrir les dépenses. Cette mémorable décision fut portée à la connaissance du conseil. Je priai instamment, dans ma lettre circulaire, les membres de faire autour d'eux une propagande active en faveur de la conférence de St. Louis. Le désir que je me permettais d'exprimer fut réalisé au-delà de toute attente. Nous étions bien éloignés d'espérer, M. Bartholdt et moi, lorsque, à Vienne, nous nous demandions combien de nos membres iraient à St. Louis, que plus de deux cent cinquante répondraient à notre appel.

Il y eut dès le commencement de l'année 1904 un échange de vues continuel entre Berne, Washington et St. Louis. Si je n'ai pas pu envoyer toujours à ceux qui m'en demandaient des renseignements précis, je les prie de considérer que la distance rendait les communications difficiles et que si je donnais des conseils ou des directions au comité américain, je devais toujours attendre ses décisions.

Le Bureau dut s'occuper aussi de la traversée, et fut l'intermédiaire entre un grand nombre de nos membres et les compagnies transatlantiques.

Le Conseil interparlementaire a tenu séance à Bruxelles, le 29 avril dernier, sous la présidence de M. Beernaert, treize membres étaient présents. Il constata le décès d'un de ses membres, don Arturo de Marcoartu, ancien sénateur espagnol, l'un des parlementaires qui s'est le plus occupé de l'arbitrage international; il en avait pour ainsi dire fait le but de son existence.

Le Conseil discuta l'organisation de la XIIe conférence et exprima plusieurs désirs concernant les arrangements à prendre par le comité américain. Il arrêta l'ordre du jour de cette Conférence et décida qu'il serait immédiatement communiqué aux groupes. Enfin, il chargea son bureau d'envoyer une adresse de félicitation aux ministres des Affaires étrangères de la France et de la Grande-Bretagne. Cette pièce fut expédiée dans la teneur suivante:

Le Conseil interparlementaire, réuni à Bruxelles le 25 avril dernier, a constaté, avec une vive satisfaction, que d'importants accords ont été conclus ces derniers temps entre la France et la Grande-Bretagne; un traité d'arbitrage d'abord, puis, tout récemment, une entente au sujet de différentes controverses qui pouvaient diviser ces deux Etats.

Par ces actes mémorables, deux puissances de premier ordre ont réalisé dans la politique internationale un progrès dont découleront les plus heureux résultats. Elles ont non seulement scellé un rapprochement qui promet d'être de longue durée, mais encore inauguré un procédé international que tous les partisans de la justice entre nations saluent comme de bon augure pour l'arbitrage obligatoire et la limitation progressive des armements. Ainsi la Grande-Bretagne et la France donnent aux autres Etats un noble exemple de grandeur d'âme qui leur assure la prépondérance morale parmi les nations et la reconnaissance de l'humanité.

Pénétré de la haute importance de ces accords, le Conseil interparlementaire, composé de délégués des parlements d'Europe et des Etats-Unis, a chargé son Bureau de présenter aux artisans des ententes franco-britanniques, ses sincères félicitations pour l'œuvre qui'ils ont si heureusement accomplie.

M. Delcassé et Lord Lansdowne ont adressé leurs remercîments au bureau du Conseil.

Le Conseil interparlementaire a tenu une seconde séance le 11 septembre à St. Louis, pour arrêter définitivement le texte des différentes résolutions proposées à la conférence.

J'aimerais pouvoir passer une longue revue des travaux et des manifestations des groupes de l'Union interparlementaire, mais il y en a peu à enregistrer.

A l'occasion de la discussion du budget par le Reichstag de l'empire d'Allemagne, M. Hoffmann, député du Wurtemberg, a développé trois points du programme des partisans de la justice internationale:

les garanties de la paix, la limitation des armements, le perfectionnement de la cour d'arbitrage de La Haye. Ces idées ne sont pas très populaires dans la patrie de Kant, et il faut un certain courage pour les aborder sur la tribune parlementaire. Cependant, elles sont déjà écoutées sans trop d'impatience. En lisant le discours de l'honorable député wurtembergeois, dans le procès-verbal du Reichstag, j'ai appris que déjà, en 1879, un de ses collègues, soumit à ce corps la proposition d'inviter le Chancelier de l'empire à faire convoquer un Congrès des Etats européens pour examiner la question de savoir s'il n'y aurait pas lieu de réduire de moitié les armements de la paix armée, provisoirement pour une durée de dix à quinze ans. Le prince de Bismarck lui répondait qu'il fallait avant tout gagner à l'idée du désarmements les voisins de l'Allemagne. Si je rappelle cet incident, qui date de vingt-cinq ans, c'est pour démontrer que les partisans du désarmement n'ont nullement lieu de se décourager. Le Chancelier impérial considérait la limitation des armements comme une utopie; vingt ans après, un Congrès universel des Etats était convoqué pour l'examiner, et s'il ne l'a pas examinée, il a tout au moins reconnu qu'elle doit l'être, et décidé qu'elle le sera dans un prochain congrès.

Dans une séance de la délégation du Reichsrat de l'empire d'Autriche, M. le docteur Licht, député, parlant comme membre de l'Union interparlementaire, a demandé que la clause d'arbitrage soit insérée dans les traités de commerce, et de telle façon que l'application en soit assurée, le tribunal arbitral devant être désigné dans la clause arbitrale. C'est, comme vous voyez, la formule votée par la Conférence interparlementaire de Vienne.

En France, M. Hubbard a demandé en séance de la Chambre des députés qu'un crédit soit inscrit au budget pour les frais de la Cour permanente de La Haye. Satisfaction lui fut donnée. Le même député a déposé à la Chambre un projet de résolution invitant le gouvernement français à se concerter avec les gouvernements étrangers pour la limitation des armements. Le ministre lui répondit que l'idée de la limitation ne rencontrera pas en France de mauvaises dispositions, mais que ce n'est pas à la France à prendre l'initiative.

Le parlement portugais continue à témoigner officiellement sa sollicitude à l'Union interparlementaire en désignant les membres des deux Chambres qui doivent en faire partie. Cette année, c'est la haute Chambre qui a désigné les soixante-un pairs et députés représentant le Parlement dans notre Union. Le Portugal se distingue d'ailleurs par sa fidélité aux principes de la justice. Une propagande considérable se fait constamment et de toutes manières dans ce pays en faveur de la paix. Ces idées sont même l'objet des cours de droit de l'université de Coimbra.

Il en est de même à Rome, du reste, où un de nos collègues, M. le sénateur Pierantoni, a fait un cours spécial sur les idées et les projets de paix et de justice internationale à travers l'histoire de l'humanité, suivi d'un commentaire des protocoles de la Conférence de La Haye.

Notre collègue, M. Wavrinsky, secrétaire du groupe suédois, a publié un rapport substantiel sur la conférence de Vienne.

J'arrive enfin à la grande république dont nous sommes aujourd'hui les hôtes.

Le Président Roosevelt, dans son message annuel au Congrès, a déclaré qu'il faut se féliciter du triomphe de l'arbitrage et qu'il est heureux de voir tant de nations se présenter devant la Cour permanente d'arbitrage de La Haye. Nous savons tous qu'il est un champion convaincu des idées de justice internationale. L'humanité lui doit que les difficultés concernant le Vénézuéla furent déférées à la Cour de La Haye, alors que les hostilités avaient déjà éclaté.

Je mentionne encore la proposition déposée par M. Bartholdt, notre collègue, à la Chambre des représentants du Congrès des Etats-Unis, invitant le Président à engager les gouvernements des nations civilisées à organiser une conférence internationale, dans le but de déterminer la conclusion de traités d'arbitrage entre les Etats-Unis et les autres nations, comme aussi de discuter l'opportunité d'une réduction graduelle des armements, et si possible, d'en arrêter les conditions. Ce serait donc la deuxième Conférence internationale prévue dans l'acte final de la Conférence de La Haye, du 29 juillet 1899.

Il me reste à établir le bilan de la justice internationale pour l'année écoulée. Depuis la Conférence de Vienne, il a été conclu des traités très importants.

C'est d'abord le traité permanent d'arbitrage entre la France et la Grande-Bretagne, suivant lequel les parties contractantes s'engagent à soumettre à la Cour permanente d'arbitrage de La Haye les difficultés d'ordre juridique ou relatives à l'interprétation des traités existant entre elles qui viendraient à se produire et qui n'auraient pu être réglées par la voie diplomatique.. Puis les accords conclus entre les mêmes Etats au sujet du Maroc, de l'Egypte, de Terre-Neuve, etc.

Viennent ensuite le traité d'arbitrage franco-italien; le traité d'arbitrage franco-espagnol; le traité d'arbitrage franco-néerlandais, tous avec la même formule que la convention anglo-française. De même, les traités conclus par la Grande-Bretagne avec l'Italie, l'Espagne, l'Allemagne, la Suède et la Norvège. De même, enfin, la convention hispano-portugaise.

Beaucoup plus large et plus général est le traité conclu entre les Pays-Bas et le Danemark, suivant lequel les parties contractantes s'engagent à soumettre à la Cour permanente d'arbitrage de La Haye tous leurs différends ou litiges qui n'auront pu recevoir une solution par la voie diplomatique. Il renferme, en outre, une clause qui ouvre à d'autres Etats la possibilité d'adhérer au traité.

Je puis ranger dans la catégorie des arrangements qui intéressent la justice internationale et le maintien des relations pacifiques entre nations, la convention franco-italienne du travail, qui a pour but d'assurer à la personne des travailleurs toutes les garanties de réciprocité, de faciliter aux nationaux travaillant à l'étranger la jouissance de leurs épargnes et l'accès aux assurances sociales, de garantir enfin aux nationaux la protection de tous leurs droits. Des différends sérieux peuvent surgir des rapports sociaux que la France et l'Italie ont réglés d'une manière qui leur fait le plus grand honneur.

Des traités d'arbitrage sont en préparation entre la Suisse, d'une part, l'Allemagne, l'Autriche-Hongrie, les Etats-Unis, la France, la Grande-Bretagne, l'Italie, d'autre part, entre le gouvernement du Canada et le Japon.

Tous ces actes sont de la plus haute importance. Ceux conclus entre la France et la Grande-Bretagne méritent surtout d'être relevés. En faisant suivre un traité d'arbitrage d'arrangements amiables au sujet de questions dont des conflits sérieux pouvaient naître, et qui ne devaient pas nécessairement être soumises à l'arbitrage, les deux gouvernements ont non seulement témoigné de leur sincère intention de maintenir entre les deux pays les relations les meilleures, mais aussi inauguré un procédé pratique qui trouvera certainement des imitateurs.

Notons encore une circonstance intéressante au point de vue de notre institution. C'est par suite de relations personnelles, amicales, semblables à celles que l'Union interparlementaire a créées et continuera de créer, que l'idée du traité d'arbitrage anglo-français a été conçue.

Il faut faire quelques réserves au sujet de la formule arrêtée entre les deux gouvernements et qui a servi de modèle à plusieurs autres conventions. La condition attachée à la clause arbitrale, si elle était interprétée dans un esprit malveillant, pourrait aisément rendre l'arbitrage illusoire. La meilleure formule, la plus sincère et la plus généreuse, est celle que le Danemark et les Pays-Bas ont choisie.

Il y a eu depuis la Conférence de Vienne les cas d'arbitrage suivants:

Canada et Etats-Unis, délimitation de frontières; Belgique et Vénézuéla, réclamation d'argent; Ecuador et Pérou, délimitation de frontières; Pérou et Colombie, délimitation de frontières.

J'allais oublier le traité général d'arbitrage, sans restriction aucune, conclu entre la République Argentine et le Chili, suivant lequel toutes les questions litigieuses qui pourraient surgir entre les deux États seront soumis à la décision du roi d'Angleterre, éventuellement du Conseil fédéral suisse. Ce dernier déclara aux parties contractantes qu'il ne pouvait pas accepter cette mission, attendu que la Suisse pouvait considérer comme son devoir d'accepter des mandats de ce genre tant que le tribunal de La Haye n'existait pas, mais qu'aujourd'hui son rôle d'arbitre est terminé.

Les autorités suisses, les premières qui aient reconnu efficacement la Cour de La Haye en décidant que toutes les difficultés résultant de l'application des traités de commerce devaient lui être soumises, se sont donc effacées devant elle en renonçant à une prérogative dont elles étaient souvent investies.

Les communications que j'ai eu l'honneur de faire à la Conférence, il y a un an, et aujourd'hui, démontrent combien sont grands les progrès de l'arbitrage international. Il ne suffit pas, à mon avis, d'en tirer la conclusion la plus immédiate, savoir qu'il y aura à l'avenir moins de contestations pouvant amener la guerre. D'autres résultats peuvent être acquis. En effet les nombreux cas d'arbitrages internationaux, les traités généraux, ou à peu près généraux, conclus entre tant de pays, les accords sur des litiges spéciaux, nés ou possibles, ont modifié considérablement les procédés politiques et diplomatiques des Etats, ainsi que les conditions de leur sécurité. Il s'est opéré évidemment des rapprochement sérieux, non seulement entre certaines nations, mais aussi d'une manière générale, et la substitution de la justice à la violence n'est plus considérée comme l'apanage et le devoir des particuliers seulement. Eh bien! si tous les différends, ou du moins la plus grande partie des différends, doivent, aux termes d'actes positifs, être réglés à l'amiable, est-il nécessaire de maintenir ce formidable appareil de la paix armée qui conduit l'Europe à la ruine? Il existe évidemment une contradiction flagrante entre les armements excessifs et les traités d'arbitrage. Le moment est donc venu d'examiner cette question, et si les gouvernements refusaient plus longtemps de le faire, ils s'exposeraient certainement au reproche que leurs accords ne sont pas sérieux.

D'autre part, les institutions naissantes de la justice internationale ont besoin de protection. Et comme, à cause de la solidarité humaine, elles sont le bien commun de toutes les nations, toutes doivent pouvoir coopérer à cette protection. De la naît la nécessité de créer, à côté de la Cour permanente d'arbitrage de La Haye, un organe chargé de faire respecter les traités, de veiller à ce que les Etats n'abusent pas des réserves contenues dans ces conventions pour substituer la violence à la justice, et, en général, de prendre dans l'intérêt commun des résolutions engageant tout au moins un certain nombre d'Etats.

Messieurs, nous nous trouvons ici sur un sol particulièrement privilégié, qui doit sa remarquable prospérité et sa prépondérance économique à deux circonstances: la fédération et l'absence d'armées permanentes. La fédération s'impose à l'Europe; elle viendra parce qu'elle doit venir. Qui pourrait taxer d'utopie les Etats-Unis d'Europe, alors que nous avons sous les yeux les Etats-Unis d'Amérique, un pays de 9 millions et demi de kilomètres carrés, aussi grand à peu près que l'Europe, un pays composé de quarante-cinq Etats, comptant près de 80 millions d'habitants? C'est l'intérêt commun qui a formé la grande république nord-américaine. Or l'intérêt commun est aussi grand, aussi accentué, dans la vieille Europe que dans la jeune Amérique et la rupture déclarée ou latente, dans l'ensemble des vingt-quatre

Etats européens, rupture qui se manifeste par l'excès de la paix armée, prouve jusqu'à l'évidence combien l'organisation politique de l'Europe est d'une absolue nécessité.

Il est ensuite procédé à la nomination des membres du Conseil interparlementaire. Sont nommés sur la proposition des groupes:

Allemagne.—Dr. Hauptmann, Dr. Max Hirsch, députés.
Autriche.—Baron de Pirquet, ancien député, S. E. v. Plener, ancien ministre.
Belgique.—MM. Beernaert, ministre d'Etat, Houzeau de Lehaie, sénateur.
Bulgarie.—MM. Bobtcheff, député, Dr. Ghennadief, ministre de la justice et député.
Danemark.—MM. v. Krabbe, député, Frédéric Bajer, ancien député.
Etats-Unis d'Amérique.—MM. Bartholdt, Burton, députés.
France.—MM. Emile Labiche, sénateur, vicomte La Batut, député.
Grande-Bretagne.—MM. Phillipp Stanhope, Randal Cremer, députés.
Hongrie.—Comte Albert Apponyi, baron Inkey, députés.
Italie.—MM. Pierantoni, sénateur, Ferraris, député.
Norvège.—MM. John Lund, ancien président du Lagting, Brandt, député.
Pays-Bas.—MM. Rahusen, sénateur, Tydeman, député.
Portugal.—MM. Dr. de Paiva, Luis B. Falcao, députés.
Roumanie.—MM. T. J. Djuvara, sénateur; Porumbaru, député.
Serbie.—MM. Nicolas Pasitch, George Simitch, conseillers d'Etat.
Suède.—MM. Ernest Beckman, Edouard Wavrinsky, députés.
Suisse.—MM. Gobat, Scherrer-Fullemann, conseillers nationaux.

L'assemblée passe à la désignation du siège de la prochaine Conférence.

M. HOUZEAU expose qu'il est désirable que les conférences aient lieu les années impaires, à cause des parlementaires américains, ceux-ci étant retenus dans leur pays les années paires; qu'il y a des offres pour 1907, mais que nous ne pouvons laisser un intervalle de trois ans entre deux conférences. En conséquence, il propose de tenir une assemblée générale en 1905 à Bruxelles, où les parlementaires recevront une hospitalité simple mais cordiale.

L'offre de M. Houzeau est acceptée avec de chaleureux remercîments. En conséquence la XIII⁰ conférence aura lieu à Bruxelles, en 1905.

L'ordre du jour étant épuisé, et personne ne demandant plus la parole, M. le président Bartholdt prononce la clôture de la XII⁰ Conférence, en annonçant aux membres, que la Conférence partira le soir même pour Denver, Chicago, le Niagara, Albany et Washington, où, le 24 septembre, elle remettra au Président Roosevelt la résolution concernant la convocation d'une deuxième assemblée générale des Etats.

M. STANHOPE remercie au nom de la conférence M. Bartholdt pour la manière dont il l'a organisée et présidée.

M. COCHERY adresse également à M. Gobat les remercîments de l'assemblée.

La séance est levée à 1 heure.

À WASHINGTON.

Les membres de la conférence sont réunis à 2 heures 30 à la Maison Blanche, dans la grande salle de réception.

M. Roosevelt, Président des Etats-Unis d'Amérique, entre accompagné de MM. Bartholdt et Gobat.

M. BARTHOLDT présente au Président les membres de la Conférence en prononçant les paroles suivantes:

Mr. President, I have the honor, as president of the Interparliamentary Union, to present to you the delegates of that organization who have attended the twelfth conference for the promotion of international arbitration, recently held at St. Louis, the first of its kind in the United States, and who are now about to return to their European homes after a tour of part of our great country, which they have made as guests of the nation and upon the special invitation of the Congress of the United States.

Fourteen different countries of Europe and, including the American Congress, fifteen parliaments of the world, are represented here by actual bearers of mandates from the people to pay their respects to you, sir, and to advise you of the purpose of their noble mission.

The Interparliamentary Union, which they represent, is composed of members of national legislative bodies who believe that peace between the several nations is just as desirable as peace between individuals of one and the same nation, and that peace can be secured and maintained by exactly the same means, namely, by arbitration. They hold, in other words, that differences between nations can and should be settled by the arbitrament of an international tribunal, the same as differences between individuals in all civilized countries are now settled by the arbitrament of local courts.

If I were permitted, on behalf of my colleagues, to further accentuate this belief, I would express it in this way: The necessity of social order requires a citizen to bow to the adjudication of the differences with his neighbor by a court of law, even when his personal honor is involved. The members of this union contend that the interests of civilization and humanity should impel each nation to do the same, no matter what may be involved, because moral as well as material rights will much more safely be vindicated by the impartial verdict of applied justice than by the results of the passionate and often blind employment of physical force. What is law for an individual should be law for a nation.

On this platform the Interparliamentary Union has grown from a small gathering of well-meaning friends of arbitration to a powerful organization, exerting its influence in all parliaments of the civilized world, the reason of its growth being, possibly, that its aims and objects are right. This organization looks upon you, Mr. President, as a friend of its cause ever since you have, by actual performance,

recognized The Hague court and had referred to it the Venezuela controversy, though you had yourself been asked to arbitrate. It is now
generally admitted that this your action, together with the Pius-fund
precedent, which also occurred under your Administration, saved the
life of that great international tribunal. The American people being
committed by these and many other precedents to the principles of
international arbitration, it is the belief of those present that the people, irrespective of party, would applaud your taking the initiative in
the convening of a second conference of governments, which we hope
and trust would result in the completion of the work begun at The
Hague, in the negotiation of further arbitration treaties, and in the
establishment of an international parliament for the consideration of
questions which are of common concern to all.

I now have the honor to introduce to you Dr. Albert Gobat, of
Switzerland, the general secretary of the Interparliamentary Union,
who will formally present to you the resolution bearing on this subject."

M. Gobat s'adresse au Président en ces termes:

Monsieur le Président, je me présente devant vous comme interprète
des sentiments de l'Union interparlementaire et j'ai l'honneur de
remettre entre vos mains une résolution votée par cette Association à
la Conférence qu'elle vient de tenir à St. Louis. Lorsqu'en 1891 nous
formulions à Rome le désir qu'il y eût prochainement un congrès de
tous les Etats civilisés, nous ne pensions pas que cette initiative serait
aussi vite suivie d'exécution, car les idées marchent lentement, du
moins en Europe. Aussi la Conférence de La Haye fut-elle une très
agréable surprise pour tous les amis de l'harmonie internationale.
Le premier aéropage des nations, malgré les difficultés qu'il rencontra,
a eu des résultats très réjouissants; il en est issu trois conventions,
dont l'une, celle concernant le réglement pacifique des conflits internationaux, est de la plus haute importance.

Malheureusement, la conférence de La Haye dut ajourner plusieurs questions qu'elle s'était proposée de discuter, notamment la plus
importante de toutes, surtout pour l'Europe, la limitation des armements. Cinq années se sont écoulées depuis lors, et personne n'a
songé à convoquer une deuxième Conférence des Etats, cette nouvelle
Conférence prévue par la convention même de La Haye du 29 juillet
1899. Initiatrice des Congrès généraux des nations, auteur intellectuel—ceci est aujourd'hui reconnu—de la Conférence de La Haye,
l'Union interparlementaire ne pouvait laisser tomber en désuétude
cette importante institution. Elle a donc décidé, le 13 septembre
dernier, à St. Louis, de réclamer la convocation d'une deuxième Conférence. Nous considérons cette institution comme le point de départ
de l'évolution la plus importante que l'humanité ait jamais faite. Car
elle donnera enfin un corps à la fraternité des peuples, à la solidarité
des intérêts intellectuels et matériels des nations, qui a toujours

existé, mais qui n'a jamais réclamé aussi impérieusement qu'aujourd'hui d'être reconnue, favorisée, protégée.

Les conférences générales des Etats règleront pour eux ce qui pour les particuliers est réglé depuis plusieurs siècles; elles rendront l'arbitrage international obligatoire; elles veilleront à la loyale observation des traités; elles préviendront les différends; elles déchargeront les peuples des charges écrasantes que de déplorables fantaisies leur imposent.   Mais cette institution, pour remplir sa mission, doit devenir aussi la base d'une organisation politique du monde.   A cet effet, il faut que les Conférences dont il s'agit soient périodiques, et, j'ajoute ici une idée personnelle, il faut qu'elles aient, dans l'intervalle de ces assemblées générales, un organe pourvu de certaines compétences de surveillance, de contrôle et d'exécution.   Ce sera la première étape d'une organisation politique internationale semblable à celle des Etats-Unis et de mon pays, la Suisse.

La Conférence interparlementaire de St. Louis a estimé que vous êtes particulièrement qualifié, Monsieur le Président, pour prendre l'initiative d'une deuxième assemblée générale.   Pareille mission appartient naturellement au chef d'un Etat où siège chaque année, là, sous la coupole du capitole, un Congrès de quarante cinq Etats.   Nous savons d'ailleurs qu'en nous adressant à vous, nous parlons à un partisan convaincu de la justice internationale et nous n'oublions pas que vous fûtes le premier chef d'Etat qui orienta le gouvernement vers la Cour permanente d'arbitrage de La Haye.   C'est donc dans l'espoir que vous voudrez bien répondre au désir de l'Union interparlementaire, et que votre initiative sera couronnée de succès, que j'ai l'honneur de vous présenter la résolution suivante:

" Whereas enlightened public opinion and the spirit of modern civilization alike demand that differences between nations should be adjudicated and settled in the same manner as disputes between individuals are adjudicated, namely, by the arbitrament of courts in accordance with recognized principles of law;

"The conference requests the several governments of the world to send representatives to an international conference, to be held at a time and place to be agreed upon by them, for the purpose of considering—

" 1. The questions for the consideration of which the conference at The Hague expressed a wish that a future conference be called.

" 2. The negotiation of arbitration treaties between the nations represented at the conference to be convened.

" 3. The advisability of establishing an international congress, to convene periodically for the discussion of international questions.

"And this conference respectfully and cordially requests the President of the United States to invite all the nations to send representatives to such a conference.

Monsieur le Président, j'ai accompli la mission officielle dont on m'a chargé.   Je me permets d'en assumer une seconde, certain que mes paroles seront ratifiées par tous les parlementaires européens. Nous vous remercions, Monsieur le Président, du fond de nos cœurs, de ce que vous ayez bien voulu joindre à l'amicale invitation adressée par le Congrès des États-Unis à l'Union interparlementaire, l'invitation de votre gouvernement et la vôtre personnelle. Nous formons les vœux les plus sincères pour le succès de vos actes politiques, pour votre bonheur et celui de votre famille, pour le bonheur et la prospérité des États-Unis, doht rien n'égale l'infini des horizons, sauf la largeur de vues et l'esprit d'indépendance des descendants de Washington et de Franklin.

M. ROOSEVELT reçut l'adresse et répondit dans les termes suivants:

Gentlemen of the Interparliamentary Union, I greet you with profound pleasure as representatives in a special sense of the great international movement for peace and good will among the nations of the earth. It is a matter of gratification to all Americans that we have had the honor of receiving you here as the nation's guests. You are men skilled in the practical work of government in your several countries; and this fact adds weight to your championship of the cause of international justice. I thank you for your kind allusions to what the Government of the United States has accomplished for the policies you have at heart, and I assure you that this Government's attitude will continue unchanged in reference thereto. We are even now taking steps to secure arbitration treaties with all other governments which are willing to enter into them with us.

In response to your resolutions, I shall at an early date ask the other nations to join in a second congress at The Hague. I feel, as I am sure you do, that our efforts should take the shape of pushing forward toward completion the work already begun at The Hague, and that whatever is now done should appear not as something divergent therefrom, but as a continuance thereof. At the first conference at The Hague several questions were left unsettled, and it was expressly provided that there should be a second conference. A reasonable time has elapsed, and I feel that your body has shown sound judgment in concluding that a second conference should now be called to carry some steps further toward completion the work of the first. It would be visionary to expect too immediate success for the great cause you are championing, but very substantial progress can be made if we strive with resolution and good sense toward the goal of securing among the nations of the earth, as among the individuals of each nation, a just sense of responsibility in each toward others. The right and the responsibility must go hand in hand. Our efforts must be unceasing, both to secure in each nation full acknowledgment of the rights of others and to bring about in each nation an ever growing sense of its own responsibilities.

At an early date I shall issue the call for the conference you request.

I again greet you, and bid you welcome in the name of the American people, and wish you Godspeed in your efforts for the common good of mankind.

Rapport du Groupe Suédois.

Le dernier rapport du groupe suédois a été présenté à la Conférence de Vienne (voir l'Appendice, annexe 1, du compte rendu de la XIe Conférence interparlementaire, 1903).

Le rapport que, par mandat de mes collègues, j'ai l'honneur de vous présenter en ce moment n'embrasse donc qu'une seule année. C'est un espace très court; mais, sans exagérer l'importance du mouvement pacifique pendant cette année, nous croyons pouvoir constater que notre cause a fait des progrès considérables.

Après avoir recueilli par les organes diplomatiques dans les divers pays des matériaux sur l'arbitrage international, le gouvernement a chargé un jurisconsulte éminent, M. Hammarskjold, président de Cour d'appel, de dresser un mémoire sur le développement de l'arbitrage et sur ses principes, de même qu'un " projet de convention," soit de traité modèle pour les conventions d'arbitrage obligatoire. Ce projet contient un article spécial suivant lequel les parties contractantes s'engagent à ne pas soulever l'exception "des intérêts vitaux, de l'indépendance ou de l'honneur national" en cas de contestations pécuniaires, lorsqu'il s'agit de l'interprétation ou de l'application des conventions de toute espèce entre les parties contractantes.

Après ces mesures préliminaires, le gouvernement entra en négociations avec certains Etats pour la conclusion de traités d'arbitrage obligatoire. Pendant ces négociations survint la déclaration anglo-française du 19 octobre 1903, par laquelle les puissances signataires ont reconnu, comme l'a exprimé la conférence diplomatique de La Haye, l'arbitrage comme le moyen le plus efficace et en même temps le plus équitable de régler les litiges.

La conclusion de traités d'arbitrage de la part de notre pays, s'étant trouvée retardée quelques mois à cause de certaines formalités, la première convention d'arbitrage obligatoire, conforme à la déclaration signée entre l'Angleterre et la France, a été conclue avec celle-ci le 9 juillet 1904 pour une durée de cinq années. Cette convention ne se borne pas à stipuler l'arbitrage pour la solution des différends, mais elle renvoie ceux-ci d'une manière obligatoire à la Cour permanente de La Haye. Comme cette convention marque une étape dans l'histoire de l'arbitrage dans notre pays, nous insérons ici le texte des articles principaux.

Article I. Les différends d'ordre juridique ou relatifs à l'interprétation des traités existant entre les Hautes Parties contractantes, qui viendraient à se produire entre elles et qui n'auraient pu être réglés par la voie diplomatique, seront soumis à la Cour permamente d'arbitrage établie par la Convention du 29 juillet 1899, à La Haye, à la condition, toutefois, qu'ils ne mettent en cause ni les intérêts vitaux, ni l'indépendance, ou l'honneur des Etats contractants, et qu'ils ne touchent pas aux intérêts de tierces puissances.

Article II. Dans chaque cas particulier, les Hautes Parties contractantes, avant de s'adresser à la Cour permanente d'arbitrage, signeront un compromis spécial, déterminant nettement l'objet du litige, l'étendue des pouvoirs des arbitres et les délais à observer, en ce qui concerne la constitution du tribunal arbitral et la procédure.

Quelques semaines après la conclusion des traités avec la France, une convention, conforme à la susmentionnée, a été conclue avec la Grande-Bretagne. Puis le gouvernement est entré en négociations pour la conclusion des traités d'arbitrage obligatoire avec le Denemark, la Belgique et les Pays-Bas. Des négociations seront ouvertes cette année dans le même but avec l'Italie, l'Espagne, le Portugal, la Suisse, puis avec les Etats-Unis de l'Amérique du Nord et les autres Etats Américains. Ces traités seront sans doute analogues à la convention du 9 juillet 1904. Cependent, on espère pouvoir introduire, dans quelques-uns, un amendement de grande importance pratique, savoir la clause dont j'ai déjà fait mention, suivant laquelle les différends d'une certaine catégorie ne seront pas considérés comme compromettant les intérêts vitaux, l'indépendance et l'honneur national.

A la conférence de Vienne, le président, M. de Plener, a signalé le rapprochement des membres des parlements anglais et français sous l'étendard de l'arbitrage comme un fait qui servira éminemment à fortifier et stimuler notre mouvement et à gagner l'opinion publique à l'idée de l'arbitrage. Ce principe est profondément enraciné chez les peuples scandinaves. Est-ce à cause de cela que notre Parlement a été honoré—le premier après celui de l'Angleterre—d'une invitation de faire une visite interparlementaire à la grande capitale de la France? Le groupe parlementaire français pour l'arbitrage international a invité cordialement les deux Chambres de notre Riksdag à se faire représenter, en même temps qu'une délégation des parlements norvégien et danois, à une réception à Paris, "une de la série de réceptions inaugurée au mois de novembre dernier par la réception en France des membres du Parlement britannique." Cette expression de la sympathie de nos collègues français, adressée aux présidents des deux chambres par l'illustre partisan de l'arbitrage, M. le baron d'Estournelles de Constant a été accueillie par le Riksdag et par la presse de notre pays avec un vif enthousiasme.

Pendant la dernière session parlementaire, notre groupe a usé de toute son influence afin de gagner des adhérents à notre union parmi nos collègues des deux chambres du Riksdag. Certes, les idées pacifiques qui inspirent l'Union interparlementaire ont bien pénétré tous les membres de notre assemblée nationale. Toutefois on ne s'est pas encore assez persuadé de la nécessité de réunir dans une association internationale tous les parlementaires qui, dans divers pays, poursuivent l'idéal pacifique: "la justice par le droit."

A l'effet de favoriser notre propagande pour l'Union interparlementaire, le groupe a continué la distribution aux membres du Riksdag des imprimés concernant l'œuvre de l'Union interparlementaire. Ainsi, on a distribué le compte rendu officiel de la XIe Conférence tenue à Vienne; un rapport, illustré, en langue suédoise sur la conférence de Vienne, rédigé par le premier secrétaire du groupe, M. Edouard Wavrinsky; une traduction du rapport du Bureau interparlementaire par le docteur Albert Gobat, etc.

Nos efforts n'ont pas été sans résultat, le chiffre des membres du groupe s'étant élevé à 117; (64 en 1902; 91 en 1903.)

Dans la réunion du groupe du 10 mai 1904, le ministre des affaires étrangères, M. Lagerheim, qui de même que les autres membres du gouvernement a toujours témoigné une vive sympathie à l'Union interparlementaire, a traité, dans un discours vivement applaudi, les principes et l'histoire des déclarations de neutralité des pays scandinaves à l'occasion de la guerre entre la Russie et le Japon.

Quelques membres du Riksdag jugeant qu'une revision de nos règles de neutralité, suivant les conceptions modernes, surtout par rapport à nos ports de guerre et à la contrebande, est d'urgence, une délégation composée de MM. Hedin, af Burén, et Wavrinsky a saisi le gouvernement d'un mémoire à ce sujet.

M. Edouard Wavrinsky, en présentant au groupe son rapport sur la séance du Conseil interparlementaire tenue à Bruxelles le 25 avril, a soumis au groupe des propositions présentées par lui au conseil, dans le but de renforcer l'Union interparlementaire et de créer des rapports plus intimes entre les groupes nationaux: chaque groupe devrait remettre au Bureau interparlementaire, chaque année, avant le mois de mars, un compte rendu de ces travaux; un résumé de ces comptes rendus serait envoyé, avant la fin du mois de septembre, au plus tard, dans un nombre suffisant d'exemplaires aux bureaux des groupes nationaux.

Le groupe suédois, depuis longtemps désireux d'avoir l'occasion de profiter des expériences des autres groupes, a donné son adhésion à une revision des statuts dans le sens de la proposition de M. Wavrinsky.

Membres du bureau pour 1904: M. Elnoson, président; M. Wavrinsky, premier secrétaire; MM. Brostrom, af Burén, Hedlund. Suppléants: MM. Beckman, J. Brunée, le comte Raoul Hamilton.

Délégués à la XIIe Conférence à St. Louis: de la première chambre, MM. Hugo Tamm, le comte Hamilton; de la seconde chambre,

MM. Beckman, von Schéck, John Olsson.   Suppléants: MM. Seb. Tham, Biesert, G. O. V. Lindgren.

Pour le groupe suédois.

EMIL BECKMAN,
Membre du Conseil interparlementaire,
président de la délégation à St. Louis.
JOHN OLSSON,
Secrétaire de la délégation.

LISTE DES MEMBRES DE LA XIIe CONFÉRENCE.

Allemagne.

Dr. Arendt, membre du Reichstag.
Prof. Hoffmann, membre du Reichstag.
M. Gerstenberger, membre du Reichstag.
Dr. Hauptmann, membre du Landtag.

Autriche.

M. le chevalier Wladimir von Oleksow Gniewosz, membre du Reichsrat, chambellan.
M. le chevalier Wladimir von Oleksow Gniewosz, fils.
Dr. baron Otakar de Prazak, membre du Reichsrat.
M. Joseph Brdlik, membre du Reichsrat.
M. Wladimir Brdlik.
M. Vaclav Karbus, membre du Reichsrat.
M. le chevalier von Duleba, membre du Reichsrat.
Prof. V. Phillippovich, membre du Landtag.
Dr. M. Baumfeld, rédacteur.

Belgique.

M. G. Francotte, ministre du travail, député.
M. Houzeau de Lehaie, sénateur.
M. le comte Goblet d'Alviella, sénateur, secrétaire du Sénat.
M. H. Bergmann, sénateur.
M. H. La Fontaine, sénateur.
M. Emile Huet, sénateur.
M. Louis de Sadeleer, député.
M. G. Helleputte, député.
M. Emile Tibbaut, député.
M. le baron Albert d'Huart, député.
M. Henry Carton de Wiart, député.
M. Emile Vandervelde, député.
M. Raymond van de Venne, député.
M. Emile Braun, député.
M. Léon Broquet, ancien député.
M. J. Carlier, ancien député.
M. Hector Van Doorslaer, greffier de la Chambre des députés.

Danemark.

M. M. C. Krabbe, vice-président de la Chambre.
M. E. Bluhme, membre du Parlement.

Etats-Unis d'Amérique.

M. Richard Bartholdt, président du groupe interparlementaire au Congrès.
M. R. E. Broussard.
M. R. R. Hitt.
M. T. E. Burton.
M. Hugh A. Dinsmore.
M. Wm. P. Hepburn.
M. Jacob Ruppert, jr.
M. Franklin E. Brooks.
M. Samuel J. Barrows.
M. Wm. A. Rodenberg.
M. James L. Slayden.
M. John Lind.

France.

M. Georges Cochery, président du groupe français, député.
M. Paul Strauss, vice-président du groupe français, sénateur.
M. le docteur Delbet, vice-président du groupe français, député.
M. Armez, député.
M. Louis Ayral, député.
M. Gustave de Bernis.
M. René Cazauvieihl, député.
M. G. Chastenet, député.
M. Georges Delesseux, membre du Conseil d'Etat.
M. Jean Desproges.
M. Alfred Duchauffour.
M. André Fallières, secrétaire général.
M. Forgemol de Bostquenard, sénateur.
M. Jacques de Geoffre de Chabrignac.
M. G. Gerald, député.
M. Louis Gotteron, sénateur.
M. le baron Georges de Grandmaison, député.
M. Janet, député.
M. Paul le Roux, sénateur.
M. le docteur Lachaud, député.
M. Pierre Larose, ancien député.
M. Adolphe Landry.
M. Mabilleau.
M. Ernest Noël, député.
M. Roch, député.
M. Rigal, député.
M. Alfred Thuillier, sénateur.
M. de Sainte-Croix, secrétaire.
M. Boucher, secrétaire.

Grande-Bretagne.

M. P. Stanhope, membre du Parlement, président du groupe.
M. W. Randal-Cremer, membre du Parlement, secrétaire du groupe.
M. S. T. Evans, membre du Parlement.
M. Corrie Grant, membre du Parlement.
M. le colonel Pryce-Jones, membre du Parlement.
M. Thos. Lough, membre du Parlement.
M. J. A. Thomas, membre du Parlement.

Dr. E. C. Thompson, membre du Parlement.
Sir Howard Vincent, membre du Parlement.
M. J. Wilson, membre du Parlement.
M. le capitaine D. V. Pirie, membre du Parlement.
M. J. Bryn-Roberts, membre du Parlement.
M. J. Caldwell, membre du Parlement.
M. Alfred Davies, membre du Parlement.
M. Fred Maddison, ancien membre du Parlement.
M. William O'Doherty, membre du Parlement.
M. T. Snape, ancien membre du Parlement.
M. W. P. Byles, ancien membre du Parlement.
Dr. G. B. Clark, ancien membre du Parlement.
M. J. W. Spear, membre du Parlement.
M. J. Jordan, membre du Parlement.
M. Arthur Priestley, membre du Parlement.
M. Herbert Whiteley, membre du Parlement.

Hongrie.

M. le comte Albert Apponyi, ancien président de la Chambre des députés, conseiller privé, chambellan du roi.
M. Aristide de Dessewffy, secrétaire du groupe hongrois.
M. Bela Kubik, député.
M. Geza de Latinovits, député.
M. Louis de Levay, ancien député.
Dr. Georges de Lukacs, ancien député.
Dr. Louis Heinrich.
Dr. Alexandre de Mohay, député, secrétaire d'Etat au ministère de la justice.
Dr. Charles Nemethy.
M. Joseph de Novak, député.
Dr. Geza de Pap, député.
M. Joseph de Piukovits, député.
Dr. Aladar Rajk, député.
Dr. Bela de Rudnyanszky, député.
M. Geza de Salamon, fils, député.
M. Bela de Barabas, député.
M. le comte Etienne Bethlen, député.
M. François Blaslovis, député.
M. Bela de Bottka, député.
M. Jules de Csorgheo, député.
M. Alexandre de Dobieczki, député.
M. Elemer de Domahidy, député.
M. Paul de Domahidy.
M. André Gyorgy, ancien député.
M. l'abbé Jean Hock, député.
M. le baron Joseph Inkey, député.
M. Léopold de Kallay, député.
M. Elemer de Kallay.
Dr. Alexandre Simonyi-Samadam, député.
Dr. Désiré de Szulyovszky, député.
M. Ferdinand d'Urmanczy, député.
M. Zoltan de Zmeskal.
M. Bela de Vermes, ancien député.

M. Ladislas de Hamory, député.
M. le comte Georges Karolyi, député.
M. François Steiner, député.
M. Aurate Csatho, rédacteur.
M. François de Komlossy, rédacteur.

Italie.

M. le marquis di San Giuliano, président.
M. le prince B. Odescalchi, vice-président, sénateur.
Prof. A. Brunialti, vice-président, député.
M. G. B. Brunialti.
M. le comte Giuseppe Bracci, député.
M. A. Capece Minutolo, Marquis di Bugnano, député.
Prof. Ettore Cicotti, député.
M. le marquis Colonel Charles Compans, député.
M. le marquis L. Compans.
M. Federico di Palma, député.
M. le colonel Arturo Galletti di Cadilhac, député.
M. Edoardo Daneo, député.
M. le comte Annibale Lucernari, député.
M. G. di Stefano, député.
M. Achille Visocchi, député.
M. A. Pavia, député.
M. le commandeur G. Cerruti, ancien député.
M. Giuseppe d'Andrea, député.
M. le marquis Théodoli di San Vito, secrétaire.

Norvège.

M. John Lund, député, président du groupe, ancien président du Lagthing.
M. Brandt, député.
M. Bernhard Hanssen, député.

Pays-Bas.

M. de Ras, ancien député.
M. M. Tydeman, député.
M. Joseph Mutsaers.
M. C. V. Gerritsen, député.
Dr. Aletta Jacobs.
M. A. Bouman, ancien député.

Portugal.

Dr. João de Paiva, ancien député.

Roumanie.

M. le général Constantin Pilat, ancien député.
M. Constantin Fotin, ancien sénateur.
M. Georges Sefendake, ancien sénateur et député.
M. Stanislas Cihoski, député.

Suède.

M. Ernst Beckman, député, président de la délégation.
M. John Olsson, député, secrétaire de la délégation.
M. G. O. v. Lindgren, député.
M. Albert Woods Beckman, rédacteur.

Suisse.

Dr. Gobat, député.
M. Ch. Kinzelbach.
M. Alfred Brustlein, député.
M. Herman Greulich, député.
M. Heinrich Scherrer, député.
Dr. Albert Studer, député.

[Translation.]

Report of Mr. Gobat, Secretary-General of the Interparliamentary Union.

A year has passed since the Conference met at Vienna. I wish to record that that meeting, of all those held heretofore, has enjoyed the greatest measure of public notice. From one end of Europe to the other, the press paid it attention and published accounts of its proceedings, generally accompanied by favorable comments. The newspapers of the capital of Austria, organs of a population that is sincerely fond of pacific aspirations, having made it a point, with remarkable zeal, for which we thank them, to give to the deliberations of the Twelfth Conference a wide publicity, the press of the other countries followed their example. I note this gratifying result in order to show how great is the importance of enlisting the interest of the newspapers at the seat of the Interparliamentary Conferences in the labors of the said Conferences. While we have thus far been unable to secure a direct cooperation of the press in our efforts, let us at least avail ourselves, for our general meetings, of the powerful means of action at its disposal. It is an auxiliary of which we stand in absolute need.

The Bureau of the Interparliamentary Union carried out the decisions of the Conference of Vienna by communicating them to the proper quarters. I then assisted in the preparation of the account of the proceedings of that meeting. The Austrian Committee had the excellent idea of taking another census of the members of the Union, the first of which I had published some ten years ago in our late magazine, "La Conférence Interparlementaire." The census shows a membership of over 2,000, not including the United States, whose group had not yet been organized. What strength lies in that figure and how much greater would that strength be, if we had a better organization!

The Peace International Bureau having called upon us to acquaint the groups of the Union with the resolutions of the Twelfth Universal Peace Congress held at Rouen, concerning the suspension of armament, the right to peace, and the use of balloons in warfare, I complied with the request and communicated the resolutions to the members of the councils.

I tried to organize a group of the Union in Greece, the only one of the European countries under a constitutional government that has not joined the institution. Having procured the addresses of several influential deputies, I made overtures to them, by sending them the reports of our proceedings, as well as the publications of the Bureau, and asked them to organize a group. One of them answered that he would do so; but thus far he has not kept his promise. The agitation now prevailing in the Balkans may account for this to a certain point.

Furthermore, the manager of the Interparliamentary Bureau, in addition to the very considerable current work that devolves upon him—his correspondence alone includes 384 letters and 8 circulars sent out since the Conference of Vienna—has had much of his time taken up by the organization of the St. Louis Conference.

That city had been conditionally designated to be the seat of our twelfth general meeting. It was agreed that the personal invitation of the American delegate to the Conference of Vienna should be confirmed by that of an Interparliamentary group. After his return home Mr. Bartholdt succeeded in organizing, in a rather short time, a group which confirmed his invitation, and I lost no time in informing the members of the Interparliamentary Union Council of the fact. Then, our honorable colleague of the United States introduced in the House of Representatives of Congress a resolution by which Congress itself was in turn to address an invitation to the members of the Interparliamentary Union. In the meanwhile I received the invitation of the American group, drawn up in accordance with all the rules. I immediately communicated it to the Interparliamentary Council. Next came the decision of Congress; a cordial invitation addressed to the Interparliamentary Union to hold its general meeting in a city of the United States, with an appropriation of the sum required to defray expenses.

This memorable resolution was made known to the council. I entreated, in my circular letter, the members to use their best efforts to promote the Conference of St. Louis. The wish, which I took the liberty of expressing, was fulfilled beyond all expectation. Mr. Bartholdt and I were far from hoping, when we wondered, at Vienna, how many of our members would go to St. Louis, that more than 250 would respond.

From the beginning of the year 1904, there was a constant exchange of views between Berne, Washington, and St. Louis. If I was not always able to send to applicants precise information, I beg them to consider that distance hampered communication and that while I offered advice or directions to the American committee, I always had to await its decision. The Bureau had also to look after the means of transportation and serve as an intermediary between a large number of our members and the ocean steamship navigation companies.

The Interparliamentary Council met at Brussels on the 29th of April last, Mr. Beernaert in the chair. Thirteen members were in attendance. It recorded the demise of one of its members, Count Don Arturo di Marcoartu, former senator of Spain, one of the parliamentarians who gave the greatest attention to international arbitration. He had made it, so to speak, the aim of his life.

The council discussed the organization of the Twelfth Conference and offered various recommendations concerning the arrangements to be made by the American committee. It framed the order of business of that conference and decided to communicate it at once to the groups. Finally it instructed its bureau to forward a congratulatory address to the ministers of foreign affairs of France and Great Britain. That paper was drawn up in the following language:

The Interparliamentary Council assembled at Brussels on the 25th of April last has noted with keen gratification that important agreements have recently been concluded between France and Great Britain, first an arbitration treaty, next, and quite recently, an agreement concerning various controversies that might arise between those two States. By these memorable acts, two powers of the first class have achieved in international policy progress from which the most happy results should flow. They have not only brought about a better understanding which bids fair to endure, but also inaugurated an international procedure which all the friends of justice among nations hail as a good omen for compulsory arbitration and the gradual limitation of armaments. Thus Great Britain and France set for the other states a noble example of magnanimity which secures to them moral preponderance among nations and the gratitude of humanity. Realizing the high importance of such agreements, the Interparliamentary Council, consisting of delegates from the parliaments of Europe and the United States, has instructed its bureau to tender to the makers of the Franco-British agreements its sincere congratulations on the work they have so happily accomplished.

Mr. Delcassé and Lord Lansdowne have addressed their thanks to the bureau of the council.

The Interparliamentary Council met again on the 11th of September at St. Louis to frame in their final shape the various resolutions laid before the council.

I should like to present a long statement of the labors and declarations of the group of the Interparliamentary Union, but there are not many to record.

On the occasion of the discussion of the budget in the Reichstag of the German Empire, Mr. Hoffmann, a deputy from Wurttemberg, set forth three points of the programme of the friends of international justice—the guaranty for peace, the limitation of armaments, the perfecting of the Court of Arbitration at The Hague. These ideas are not very popular in Kant's fatherland, and it requires some courage to broach the subject in Parliament. Yet they are even now listened to without excessive impatience. By reading the speech of the honorable deputy from Wurttemberg and the Record of the Reichstag, I learned that, as far back as 1879, one of his colleagues introduced a resolution requesting the Chancellor of the Empire to call a congress of the European States for the purpose of examining the question whether it would not be expedient to reduce by one-half the armaments of armed peace, provisionally, for a term of ten or fifteen years. Prince Bismarck answered him that the first thing to do was to win the neighbors of Germany over to the idea of disarming. My purpose in mentioning this incident, which occurred twenty-five years ago, is to show that the friends of disarmament have no occasion to feel discouraged. The Imperial Chancellor looked upon the limitation of armaments as an impracticable scheme. Twenty years later a Universal Congress of the States was called to consider the question; and while it has not done so, it has at least admitted that it should be, and decided that it shall be, so examined by a future congress.

At a sitting of the Reichsrat delegation of the Empire of Austria, Doctor Licht, deputy, speaking as a member of the Interparliamentary Union, asked that the arbitration clause be inserted in commercial treaties, and in such a way that its enforcement be secured by designating the Tribunal of Arbitration in the arbitral clause. This, as you see, is the formula adopted by the Interparliamentary Conference of Vienna.

In France, Mr. Hubbard asked, at a session of the Chamber of Deputies, that an appropriation be made for the maintenance of the permanent court at The Hague. He carried his point. The same deputy introduced in the chamber a resolution requesting the French Government to concert with foreign governments arrangements for the limitation of armaments. The minister replied that the idea of limitation would not meet in France with serious opposition, but that it was not for France to take the initiative.

The Portuguese Parliament continues to give official evidence of its interest in the Interparliamentary Union by designating the members of both houses who are to belong to it. This year it was the Upper House that designated the 61 peers and deputies representing the Parliament in our Union. Portugal distinguishes itself by its loyalty to the principles of justice. Sentiment favorable to peace is largely, constantly, and in every manner promoted in that country. These ideas are even made the subject of law lectures in the University of Coimbra. Similar conditions exist at Rome also, where one of our colleagues, Senator Pierantoni, delivered special lectures on the ideas and projects of international peace and justice throughout the history of mankind, followed by a commentary on the protocols of the conference of The Hague.

Our colleague, Mr. Wavrinsky, secretary of the Swedish group, has published a detailed report of the Conference of Vienna.

I now come to the Great Republic, of which we are now the guests.

President Roosevelt in his annual message to Congress declared that the triumph of arbitration is a matter for congratulation, and that he was happy to see so many nations appear before the Permanent Court of Arbitration at The Hague. We all know that he is an earnest defender of the idea of international justice. Humanity owes it to him that the difficulties concerning Venezuela were laid before the Court of The Hague after hostilities had already broken out.

I will also mention the resolution introduced in the Congress of the United States by our colleague, Mr. Bartholdt, in the House of Representatives, requesting the President to invite the governments of civilized nations to organize an international conference for the purpose of bringing about the conclusion of arbitration treaties between the United States and the other nations, as well as of discussing the expediency of a gradual reduction of armaments and of determining the conditions thereof, if possible. This would then be the second international conference contemplated in the final act of the Conference of The Hague of July 29, 1899.

I now have to present a statement of the acts of international justice for the past year. Since the Conference of Vienna, very important treaties have been concluded.

First, the permanent treaty of arbitration between France and Great Britain, by which the contracting parties bind themselves to refer to the Permanent Court of Arbitration at The Hague all difficulties of a juridical order or relative to the interpretation of treaties in force between them that may arise and can not be adjusted through the diplomatic channel.

The agreements concluded between the same States concerning Morocco, Egypt, Newfoundland.

Next come the Franco-Italian arbitration treaty;

The Franco-Spanish arbitration treaty;

The arbitration treaty between France and the Netherlands;

All framed in the same language as the Anglo-French convention.

Likewise the treaties concluded by Great Britain with Italy, Spain, Germany, Sweden and Norway.

Likewise, and lastly, the convention between Spain and Portugal.

The treaty concluded between the Netherlands and Denmark is of a much broader and more general character. The contracting parties bind themselves to submit to the Permanent Court of The Hague all their differences and disputes that can not be settled through the diplomatic channel. It also contains a clause which makes it possible for other States to adhere to the treaty.

I may class among arrangements of interest to international justice and the maintenance of pacific relations among nations the Labor Convention between France and Italy, whose object is to guarantee reciprocally personal safety to the laboring men, to facilitate to their respective citizens working away from home the enjoyment of their savings and access to mutual benefit societies, and finally to secure for them the protection of all their rights. Serious differences may arise from social relations which France and Italy have adjusted in a manner that does them both great honor.

Arbitration treaties are being prepared between Switzerland, on the one hand, Germany, Austria-Hungary, the United States, France, Great Britain, Italy, on the other hand, and between the Governments of Canada and of Japan.

The greatest importance attaches to all these acts. Those concluded between France and Great Britain especially are worthy of mention. By following up an arbitration treaty with amicable agreements concerning questions from which serious conflicts might spring, and which were not necessarily to be submitted to arbitration, the two Governments have not only given evidence of their sincere intention to maintain the best relations between the two countries, but have also inaugurated a practical procedure which will certainly find imitators.

Let us here note an interesting circumstance, from the standpoint of our Institution. The idea of the arbitration treaty between France and Great Britain sprang from and was a consequence of friendly personal relations like those which the Interparliamentary Union has created and will continue to create.

Some reservation must be made in regard to the formula adopted by the two Governments which has been used as a model for several other conventions. The condition attached to the arbitration clause might, if interpreted in an unfriendly spirit, easily make arbitration nugatory. The best, the most sincere, the most generous formula is that which Denmark and the Netherlands have selected.

Since the Conference of Vienna the following cases of arbitration have taken place:

Canada and the United States, demarkation of boundaries.

Belgium and Venezuela, indemnity claim.

Ecuador and Peru, demarkation of boundaries.

Peru and Colombia, demarkation of boundaries.

I came near forgetting the general treaty of arbitration, without any restriction whatever, concluded between the Argentine Republic and Chile, under which all disputes that may arise between the two States shall be submitted to the decision of the King of England, eventually to that of the Swiss Federal Council. The latter notified the contracting parties that it could not accept that office, inasmuch as while Switzerland might have deemed it her duty to accept such duties as long as the tribunal of The Hague was not in existence, her rôle of arbitrator was now at an end.

The Swiss authorities, which were the first to give effective recognition to the court of The Hague by deciding that all difficulties arising from the enforcement of commercial treaties should be submitted to it, have thus given way to it by relinquishing a prerogative with which they had been repeatedly vested.

The communications I have had the honor to make the Conference, a year ago and to-day, show how great the progress of international arbitration has been. It is not enough, in my opinion, to draw therefrom the most immediate conclusions, namely, that there will be in the future fewer disputes apt to bring about a war. Other results may be achieved. Indeed, the numerous cases of international arbitration, the general, or nearly general, treaties concluded between so many countries, the agreements reached on special disputes, actual or likely, have considerably modified the political and diplomatic procedure of the States, as well as the conditions of their safety. It is evident that not only a much better understanding has been effected among certain nations, but also, that it is generally prevalent, and that the substitution of justice for violence is no longer considered as the privilege and duty of the private individual only. Now if all differences, or at least the greater part of differences, must, under positive covenants, be settled amicably, is it necessary to maintain the formidable equipment of armed peace which is leading Europe to her ruin? There obviously exists a flagrant contradiction between excessive armament and arbitration treaties; so the time has come to examine this question, and if governments should still decline to do so they would surely lay themselves open to the reproach that their agreements are insincere.

On the other hand, the new-born institutions of international justice require protection, and, inasmuch as by reason of human solidarity they are the common property of all nations, all should be able to cooperate in extending such protection. Thence arises the necessity of creating, by the side of the Permanent Court of Arbitration at The Hague, an organ charged with the duty of enforcing the treaties, of seeing to it that States shall not abuse the reservations contained in these conventions with a view of substituting violence for justice, and, in a general way, of passing, in the general interest, resolutions binding on a certain number of the States at least.

Gentlemen: We are here on a particularly privileged land, which owes its remarkable prosperity and its financial preponderance to two circumstances—federation and the absence of standing armies. Europe must have federation; it will come, because it is bound to come. Who could call the United States of Europe a Utopian notion when we have before our eyes the United States of America, a country of nine and a half millions of square kilometers, nearly as large as Europe, a country consisting of forty-five States, with a population of nearly eighty millions? Mutual interests gave birth to the great Republic of North America. Now, mutual interests are as great, as pronounced, in Old Europe as in Young America, and the open or latent rupture among the twenty-four European States, which is made apparent by excessively armed peace, affords evidence of the absolute necessity of political organization for Europe.

O